THE BIBLE
THROUGH ASIAN EYES

D1615858

THE BIBLE
THROUGH ASIAN EYES

Masao Takenaka and Ron O'Grady

Pace Publishing

in association with

Asian Christian Art Association

© Asian Christian Art Association 1991

The Bible Through Asian Eyes
First published 1991:

Pace Publishing,
P.O. Box 15.774,
Auckland 7, New Zealand.

In association with:
The Asian Christian Art Association,
Kansai Seminar House, 23 Takenouchi-cho, Ichijoji,
Sakyo-ku, Kyoto 606, Japan.

Set in 10/11 Palatino
Printed by Art Attack, Hong Kong.

ISBN: 0-9597971-0-6

All scripture quotations are from the Good News Bible (The Bible in Today's English Version).
New Testament © American Bible Society, New York 1966,1971 and 4th edition 1976.
Old Testament © American Bible Society, New York, 1976.
British usage edition © British and Foreign Bible Society, Swindon, 1976. Used with permission.

Distributors:
World Council of Churches, 150 Route de Ferney, 1211 Geneva 20, Switzerland.
Christian Conference of Asia, 57 Peking Road, Kowloon, Hong Kong.
Joint Board of Christian Education, 10 Queen Street, Melbourne, Vic. 3000, Australia.
Friendship Press, P.O. Box 37844, Cincinnati OH 45222-0844, United States of America.

Contents

Introduction

After many years of planning, it is a great joy to introduce another book on Asian Christian art. This new collection has the evocative title: *The Bible Through Asian Eyes* by which we mean the eyes of Asian artists. Does this mean that Asian eyes are different from those in other parts of the world? Do Asians see the Bible in a particular way? The answer to that question is both yes and no. The Bible speaks universal words of life which are the same wherever they are read. But the context in which those words are read, imagined and interpreted differs from one culture to another.

The slum dweller in Manila who has never seen a sheep has problems when told that Jesus is the good shepherd. How does the person whose staple food is rice understand the phrase, "our daily bread"? Our situation determines our perception; the cultural habitat of our lives gives us a unique way of seeing the world.

This is certainly true of visual art. Dr Masao Takenaka points out the distinctive way in which many people in Asia view a painting:

> "Traditional Oriental painting stresses the importance of listening in visual art. Certainly life in the atmosphere, in nature, in a sanctuary or in a tea house is mobile and liquid. It has colour and shape which we see. But if we 'see' only what we have seen, then we would be aware only of the external technique and surface reality.
>
> The Oriental approach to art emphasizes the art of listening, even in the case of visual art. This may appear strange. Is not visual art, 'visual'? In it we normally stress the colour and the form of the object."

It is a particularly Asian gift to ask if "we see only what we see." Beiu Iizuka, one of the leaders in black and white Oriental painting *nanga* has said:

> "While Western painting stresses colour and shape, Eastern painting emphasizes the voice. When we see the waterfall we listen to the sound of the waterfall. When we see the birds we listen to the singing of the birds. When we see a flower, we listen to the song of the flower."

It seems clear that when we stand before a work of art even our perception of what is being portrayed differs according to our own cultural background and experience. Asian eyes may indeed have a unique way of viewing reality which will help others to see familiar things in a new perspective.

The contemporary context in which Asians paint, sculpt, sing and write Christian art is also markedly different from that of their brother and sister artists in the West. Asia is still, for the most part, suffering economic hardship. The largest number of absolutely poor people in the world are still to be found in Asia. (Six hundred million according to recent World Bank estimates). To people with sensitivity, the existence of so many of their neighbours in extreme poverty is shocking and incomprehensible.

In recent history Asians have suffered the humiliation of colonialism or foreign occupation and this has been followed by the exhilaration of apparent freedom and independence. Many of the artists and poets in this book have been on the frontier of the struggle for national independence and their interpretation of the Bible has been deeply influenced by the social context in which they have been placed.

It is the religious environment of Asia which makes this collection of art so unique. Christianity is an ancient religion - even in Asia its history can be traced back almost two thousand years to the time of the apostles - but the strength of indigenous religions meant that the growth of the Christian faith in Asia was negligible for centuries. Even today, despite considerable church growth in some countries, Christians number less than 10% of the total Asian population and in several countries the numbers are less than 1%.

Asia remains the heart of the world's great religions. Hinduism, Islam, Buddhism, Shintoism and numerous smaller religions had their beginnings on Asian soil and still exert a powerful influence on society. To be a Christian artist in such a setting means coming to terms with the art forms and images of other religions. Artists in Asia struggle with questions which are not even contemplated by Western artists. Jyoti Sahi of India, a theologian and artist, has given prominence to these questions for Christians in India. He writes:

"Christians have a special feeling that Jesus belongs to them. When one represents Jesus, baptized Christians immediately have a sense that in some way the image *belongs* to them. What I would like to suggest here is that the image of Jesus is an authentic expression of *non-Christians*. When Jamini Roy or K.C.S. Paniker (both are Hindus) represented Jesus they were not crypto-Christians. It appears to me that a Buddhist, Hindu, Moslem or even an agnostic can represent Jesus as an authentic expression of his or her belief. That is, the image of Jesus can represent a true confession of faith for a believing Hindu, Buddhist or Moslem. Jesus can be experienced by men and

Jamini Roy: Crucifixion

"The image of Jesus can represent a true confession of faith for a believing Hindu, Buddhist or Moslem." (Jyoti Sahi)

women of all religions.

This I feel, is the unique prophetic message of art in Asia - that it can witness to a dialogue between religions, where dialogue is vital for peace. This art challenges our usual compartments, by being universal in its confession of truth."

To those unfamiliar with Asia, it may seem strange that artists who are active members of another religion would want to paint Christian themes. But the reality is that many great art works on Christian themes have been painted by people of other faiths. A few of these have been included in this book. A Buddhist monk from Sri Lanka, Ven Hatigammana Uttarananda, has been so influenced by Christian teaching that most of his paintings are now based on the Bible even though he remains a Buddhist priest.

There is a similar phenomena in the West. Arguably the most important New Zealand artist this century is Colin McCahon who died in 1987. He was constantly returning to the Bible for words and images which could be used in his art. Yet for all his deep knowledge of the Bible and concern to represent the Christian message, he was not a member of the church.

This brings us to the basis for selecting the art contained in this book. The Asian Christian Art Association decided to proceed with the publication of a collection of art works on the Bible with the provision that three criteria be maintained:

1. The art work must be of high professional quality.
2. It must deal with a recognizable Biblical theme.
3. It should have an "Asian character" of expression.

The editors set to work to sift through a mountain of possible art works. Well over 1000 art works were considered for publication and, after much consideration these were reduced to the final 100 art works which appear in this volume.

There has been no attempt to select art works which emphasize one particular style of art such as traditional, realism, abstract. The artists have their own integrity and their personal choice of medium and style is motivated by a number of other factors.

For example, there are several Asian artists searching their own nation's cultural history to find an authentic indigenous basis for their art. Ketut Lasia uses the disciplined Balinese style of art to paint Biblical stories; Australian Aboriginal artists draw on symbols which are thousands of years old to portray the Biblical

Ketut Lasia: The Lord's Supper
Art and life are synonymous.

message; Kim Hak Soo and Kim Ki Chang have found inspiration in Korean folk art; many Chinese artists are using brush painting and promising young artists from Thailand and Burma, Sawai Chinnawong and Saw Edward, are exploring the traditional art styles of their countries. Many Asian Christian artists believe that the use of indigenous art enables them to communicate Biblical messages more directly with their own people.

There are fundamentalist Christians who find the depiction of Christ in an indigenous setting irreverent, or at least hard to accept, but the paintings challenge the viewer to recognise the universality of Christ and can expose us to a new understanding of Christ as the person who speaks all languages in all cultures.

In making the selection, the editors were again impressed by the high standard of Christian art in Asia. At a time when Christian art in the West appears to be dormant and in some places under attack from modern iconoclasts, it is gratifying to know that it is alive and full of energy in Asia. The artist is still honoured and respected in many Asian cultures.

It was particularly good to discover that an increasing number of women artists are now being accepted in the Asian art world where they are making their own unique contribution.

Art has not yet been fully commercialised in Asia. It is still seen as an integral part of daily life and in many communities there is no specific word for "art." In a society such as Bali, art and life are synonymous so that part of the education of every child is to bring out the artist that lives within them. In this context the visual expression of Christianity, compared to its verbal expression, communicates much more directly.

In modern China, the role of the artist has developed special importance. During the cultural revolution, the church in China was often under attack for being too "Western." There is a degree to which this criticism was valid. In most countries, missionaries to Asia brought Western cultural values hand-in-hand with the Christian gospel so that the two often seemed fused together. To be a Christian in Asia became synonymous with rejecting one's traditional clothes for western garb, singing hymns to foreign music and worshipping in stone buildings unsuited for tropical climates. In modern China, the credibility of the church lies in it being faithful to its own cultural roots. This is nowhere more evident than in the arts and it is no accident that musicians and artists in China are now playing a crucial role in pointing the Chinese church in a new direction.

He Qi, an art instructor at the Nanjing Theological Seminary, writes:

"In recent years, our Nanjing Seminary art classes, professors, students and many sympathetic and enthusiastic friends in the art world, together with the concern and support of Bishop K.H. Ting and the entire Seminary body, have been exploring and experimenting in the task of indigenization of Chinese Christian art. A number of ink and wash paintings, papercuts, woodcuts and other works in various folk styles have been produced. We hope that our work will add something to the richness of the ecumenical church, and for this we are willing to work and search tirelessly."

In the preparation of this book, the editors received constant encouragement from leaders of the Chinese church. Bishop Ting wrote that he is greatly interested in the publication and he has encouraged artists from his country to participate.

There is a vitality in the Chinese quest for an indigenous Christian expression that will eventually benefit the whole Christian world.

In 1975 the first volume of *Christian Art in Asia*, edited by Professor Masao Takenaka, was published in association with the Christian Conference of Asia. It was a pioneering work and created so much interest that an Asia-wide conference of artists was held in Bali, Indonesia in 1978. Out of this gathering, the Asian Christian Art Association was formed.

Recent years have seen considerable growth in the number of Asian artists painting Biblical themes and a noticeable improvement in the overall quality of Christian art. The Association has played its part in this growth by giving greater visibility to artists and providing a forum through which artists have access to a wider audience. Asian Christian art has developed in recent years to such an extent that the Association decided it was time to produce a new volume of works by Asian artists. In choosing the theme of the Bible through Asian eyes, the Association opted for a publication which will have wide appeal to churches around the world. The book has been designed to be a companion volume to *Christian Art in Asia* and together the two books record the development of Christian art in the Asian region.

We are particularly grateful to the many people who have supported this publication. Evangelisches Missionswerk and Missio in Germany, the Mission and Worldservice desk of the Reformed Churches in the Netherlands, the United Church of Canada, the Church of Sweden Mission and the Suntory Foundation of Japan

He Qi: The Good Samaritan - Paper Cut
*"We hope that our work will add something to the richness of
the ecumenical church." (He Qi)*

have given practical support toward this publication. To them we express our appreciation.

In the selection of reflections to complement the art works we have been assisted by a number of Asian writers, some of whom wrote a meditation specially for this publication. Their work helps to give this book its uniquely Asian character.

Above all we owe a special debt to the artists who willingly permitted us to use their works in this book. Their vision of Asian society based on Christian values interpreted through art is a prophetic ministry which helps us all to understand the future.

At the 1984 Manila Conference of the Asian Christian Art Association, the chairman, Dr Takenaka, opened the gathering with a prayer which contained these words:

> "Help us to open our eyes of understanding to perceive the mystery of your creation and to make a fitting response with the imaginative gift you have given each of us. Sustain and encourage a community of artists in Asia who will share their aspirations in Jesus Christ. Help the artists to be humble in accepting the illuminating light and be courageous and creative in expressing the promise of freedom.
>
> Being inspired by them, may each one of us also become a kind of artist so that we can respond to your word creatively."

This is an appropriate dedication with which to begin this book.

❏

The Old Testament

Creation

In the beginning, when God created the universe, the earth was formless and desolate. The raging ocean that covered everything was engulfed in total darkness and the power of God was moving over the water. (Genesis 1: 1,2)

One of the oldest creation stories comes from the *Rig Veda*, a collection of hymns in India. The creation hymn bears the title: "Who Can Say Whence It All Came and How Creation Happened?"
"Then there was neither death nor immortality,
nor was there then the torch of night and day.
The One breathed windlessly and self-sustaining.
There was that One then; and there was no other.
Whence all creation has its origin,
he, whether he fashioned it or whether he did not,
he, who surveys it all from highest heaven,
he knows - or maybe he does not know."

"The words of Genesis 1:1 must not be understood simply to mean the creation of the cosmos. It is in truth the beginning of history. It declares that God in freedom, without any coercion, exercised freedom and created the heavens and the earth. These opening words from the book of Genesis are God-centred, eschatalogical words. It is in this God that the worlds of nature and history are united. The moment God created the heavens and the earth - the moment we confess this - history has begun. When we say, 'in the beginning God...' we are to see the meaning of the heavens and the earth in the light of God. It is important to know that this God does not use freedom for the satisfaction of greed. The Creator God is a self-giving God. God rejects greed. This is the meaning of history. And in this rejection is the possibility of right appreciation of nature. We come to a new understanding of history when we see it in the light of the God who rejects greed." - Kosuke Koyama, Japan / USA

Love is revealed in words
When words are not enough,
  it is revealed in deeds.
When deeds are not enough,
  love resorts to music.
Creation is the music of God.
  - Indian proverb

Edgar "Egai" Fernandez was born in the Philippines in 1955. After studying fine arts, he showed enough promise to begin painting professionally.
Inspired by the struggle for freedom in his country he became active in Concerned Artists of the Philippines, a group using their talents for social change. Like many in the group, he developed a style of social realism which had a popular appeal among ordinary people.
A strong supporter of the Asian Christian Art Association, he is currently Coordinator-at-large of the Association and often travels to talk with artists in other countries. His series of works on "Creation" was shown in May 1990 at Gallery Genesis in Manila. The first work in the series shows the child in space in the moment of creation. A ribbon in the child's hand forms a dove symbolising the hope for peace which was there in the hearts of all people at the beginning.

Egai Fernandez: In the Beginning

Creation - Day Three

Then God commanded, "Let the earth produce all kinds of animal life: domestic and wild, large and small" - and it was done. So God made them all, and he was pleased with what he saw. (Genesis 1:24,25)

"In the process of creation, God emphasized the word 'good' again and again, no matter what - the light, the darkness, the water, the land, the plants, the animals, humans and other creatures. God was satisfied with all his creation.

After he created human beings, he placed them in the garden of Eden and they lived harmoniously with animals, plants and nature. The situation was wonderful. Nature which is made by God always manifests God's power. God manifests himself in nature. Moses encountered God in the wilderness. God proclaimed the ten commandments on the mountain and set the rainbow in the clouds to be a sign of his covenant with humans. The clear waters, the cool stream, the beautiful sunset, all manifest the beauty of nature. Poets and painters catch their inspiration from nature. We affirm that nature is good...

God's command to humans is to 'rule over' the sea, the air and every living creature that moves on the ground. How do we define 'rule over' since humans cannot conquer nature? It is obvious that the responsibility of humankind is to take care of God's creation, but humankind has neglected this responsibility. Creation is continually being destroyed and if this continues, humankind will be banished from the beautiful garden again...

Today, if we are to 'make disciples' there should be a relationship not only between God and humankind, between human and human, but between human beings and nature as well. Every Christian must become the voice of conscience, providing the way for justice and leading a development that is in contact with theology. Our faith calls us to pursue God's justice, God's peace and God's righteousness.

- Chuang Su-Jen, Taiwan

TawanDuchanee was born in Thailand, 1939. He studied at Amsterdam University, Netherlands where he received a UNESCO award at the Royal Academy of Art. He has painted a number of works on creation including a mural at the Student Christian Centre in Bangkok.

Tawan Duchanee: Creation

Creation - Day Seven

And so the whole universe was completed. By the seventh day God finished what he had been doing and stopped working. He blessed the seventh day and set it apart as a special day, because by that day he had completed his creation and stopped working.
(Genesis 2: 1-3)

When Leonard French conceived the idea of painting a creation series, he planned to conclude it with a circle. He commented, "All the days became one and everything was alive on earth."

The painting is filled with the powerful symbolism of cross and circle. At its heart lies a circular tiled garden surrounded by the cross. The sun, moon and stars are on the vertical and the hands of blessing, or suffering, on the horizontal. The outer circle has two reclining figures in the midst of created life - fish, birds and plants, held together in the symmetry of the circle.

The circle is the basic religious symbol and draws together both outer and inner life. In its completion it holds together the universe.

The haloes of saints, rose windows of cathedrals, circles drawn by zen masters, the wheel of the law in Buddhism, mandalas of artists and the circle of The Seventh Day all speak of perfect wholeness and holiness. They symbolise the life of perfect harmony, complete and abundant.

Leonard French was born in Melbourne in 1928 and has become one of Australia's leading artists. His work is identified by a powerful set of symbols, colours and techniques that set him apart from other artists of his generation. "The Seven Days" (of creation) painted in enamel on hessian-covered hardboard is owned by the Australian National University in Canberra. It is one of his most important works with highly textured surface of moulded symbols, string, gold leaf and enamel.

In 1961 French was holidaying with his family in Greece where he experienced the mystic drama of Byzantine iconic images. One day in the summer of 1962 his son swam out through the clear water and asked his father, "how did the world begin?" The paintings were the father's attempt to answer his son's question.

The fifth day (left) sees the man breaking free "garbed in the rituals his life will bring". A chasuble shape carries symbols of creation with the chi-rho monograph of Christ in the centre. The serpent's power is broken at this new birth. The works in the Creation series are enamel on hardboard.

The Seventh Day (opposite) is a 4.3 metre circle.

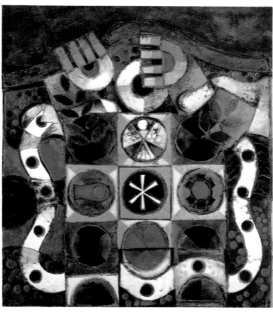

The Fifth Day

Leonard French: The Seventh Day

Adam and Eve

Now the snake was the most cunning animal that the Lord God had made. The snake asked the woman, "Did God really tell you not to eat fruit from any tree in the garden?"
"We may eat the fruit of any tree in the garden," the woman answered, "except the tree in the middle of it. God told us not to eat the fruit of that tree or even touch it; if we do, we will die." The snake replied, "That's not true; you will not die. God said that, because he knows that when you eat it you will be like God and know what is good and what is bad."
(Genesis 3: 1-5)

We are losing paradise
to the dollar and the yen
To the money lender's guile
and the wealthy banker's pen.

And our hope of finding Eden
is fast fading from our mind
 with the ethics of consumption
and the morals of the blind.

But Adam is persistent
And Eve will find a way
For tomorrow to be better
than our dreams of yesterday.

Paradise Lost (Detail)

Abubakar was born in 1930 in the Palmas region of South Sulawesi. He was born into a Moslem family but educated at a Christian School. A self-taught artist, his art has often used Christian themes as the only ones adequate to express his understanding of human suffering. Genesis and its stories of creation were a popular subject for his art. In 1980 he painted the temptation of Adam and Eve on canvas (opposite) and later a larger series on paradise lost (detail left). He sees the lost paradise as the result of our own deeds and not as a punishment from God. "It is the karma of our own deeds", he says, "to lose paradise or regain it."
He continues to experiment with several techniques including batik, woodcut, monoprint, watercolours and woodcarving.
He now lives in Jakarta and assists church publishing programmes.
"I still see myself as a pilgrim," he writes."I am still seeking after truth and beauty, and how to show God's love in my life and my art."

Abubakar: Adam and Eve

Eve

The woman (Eve) saw how beautiful the tree was and how good its fruit would be to eat, and she thought how wonderful it would be to become wise. So she took some of the fruit and ate it. (Genesis 3: 6)

Eve found a tree
With beautiful fruits
Legended to give knowledge
Of good and evil
Of God the Omni-scient

I want to be wise
I want to be a person of myself
Knowing all and being empowered
Nor being ordered neither dependent
Not even on God, the Controlling Almighty

I want to use good sense of mine
And pursue the infinite realm
Of knowing to have access
To the governance
Of life of mine and my people
Expanding our world to the boundless bountiful
And to the horizons of eternity

Eve took the fruits and ate
And she gave some to her husband
Without reasoning Adam ate
And he became knowledgeable
As much as Eve

But ever since it is Adam
Who monopolizes the power of knowing
For his reasoning has become
More radically capacitated than his wife
Who was wiser than he in the beginning

But Eve, even in her forced subjugation
Still holds Godly pride and self-esteem
Fit to be the image of the Creator

And human history
Unfolds into modernity.
                    - Sun Ai Lee Park, Korea

Yasutake Funakoshi was born in 1912 and after study in the Tokyo Art Academy specialised in sculpture. His best-known work is the powerful "Twenty-six Martyrs of Nagasaki", unveiled in 1962, which stands outside the memorial building at Nagasaki. He taught at the Tokyo University of Art for many years and produced religious works of art during that time.
An active Roman Catholic he has inherited the spiritual heritage of his father who was the first convert to Christianity in his family.
His bronze casting of Eve was completed in 1986.

Yasutake Funakoshi: Eve

The Great Flood

When the Lord saw how wicked everyone on earth was and how evil their thoughts were all the time, he was sorry that he had ever made them and put them on the earth. He was so filled with regret that he said, "I will wipe out these people I have created, and also the animals and the birds, because I am sorry that I made any of them." (Genesis 6: 5-7)

Indonesian artist Sudjojono was walking along a Jakarta street when he passed a young prostitute. She was so young and fresh and beautiful that he had to contrast this with her choice of an occupation that would destroy her.

He went home and painted her with red lips and hands clasped in prayer. He visualised her living in the time of Noah and sinking beneath the waves of the great flood. As she drowns she is given an insight into the reality of God which she had never known before. She cries out -

"Lord, you are present
You are very real to me now
May I stretch out my hand
And touch you?"

Sudjojono reminds us of another prostitute of whom Jesus said, "the great love she has shown proves that her many sins have been forgiven." (Luke 7:47)

"Later generations, especially those of the twentieth century, have often held the promise (of the covenant with Noah) aloft as a protection, not against disaster and famine, but against their own greed and exploitation of the earth. Their argument goes like this...'We have God's promise. While the earth lasts, seedtime and harvest, cold and heat, summer and winter, day and night, shall never cease. And see, the rainbow is there to remind us of God's protection.'

Yet along with the tide of people who have needed no theology to back up their actions and their ideas of progress, where has such thinking led to? Industrialized nations, building on western notions of development and the equation that materialism equals progress, have brought the earth to the brink of disaster."

 - Rosemary Russell, Aotearoa/New Zealand

*S. **Sudjojono** is respected as the father of modern Indonesian painting. When he was 24 years of age he organised a group of young Indonesian artists into a union. They became known as Persagi and were a powerful force in bringing an artistic renaissance to Indonesia. When the revolutionary war against the Dutch took place, Sudjojono said that "he used his brush as a weapon" and became an active leader in the independence struggle. In 1949 he painted his huge and impressive work "The Hour of the Guerilla."*

Elected to the Indonesian parliament in 1955 he became disillusioned with corruption in politics and was expelled from the party in 1958.

A passionate worker for peace and justice. Sudjojono kept returning to Biblical symbols to express his convictions.

Several of his paintings were based on the story of Noah with its overtones of the destruction of humanity because of their sin. His oil painting of the prostitute in the flood was painted for the inaugural conference of Asian Christian artists in Bali.

Sudjojono died in 1986 at the age of 69 years.

Sudjojono: The Flood

The Ark of Noah

(God said to Noah) "Build a boat for yourself out of good timber; make rooms in it and cover it with tar inside and out."... Noah was six hundred years old when the flood came on the earth. He and his wife, and his sons and their wives, went into the boat to escape the flood. A male and a female of every kind of animal and bird, whether ritually clean or unclean, went into the boat with Noah, as God had commanded. Seven days later the flood came. (Genesis 6: 14, 7: 6-10)

God asked a man to make an ark
and man made an ark,
The ark became a symbol
of God's house
and in it man gathered for God
all the living beings.

There was a flood
and the ark became home
for humankind, for the beast,
and for the fowl.

Man sent a dove to find out
if the flood calmed down
if the rain stopped and
if the winds became tame.

The dove returned
with an olive branch.
The dove and the olive branch
they became symbols of peace.

'May all the peoples of the earth
live in peace'.
thus prayed the ancient sages
of my land.

> — Solomon Raj, India

Solomon Raj was born in a small village in South India and educated at Lutheran schools. After taking a Master's degree in communication at Indiana University he returned to India and worked for several years with the Indian Church's Audio Visual Department (CARAVS) in Madras.
A versatile communicator, he has written radio plays and musicals based on Biblical themes and in his visual art he is best known for his woodblock prints and batiks.
In 1984 he completed a doctoral thesis on Christian folk religion in India.
He writes: "In my country we Christians are a minority, and so we find that we must preach the gospel and convey our faith to our Hindu brothers and sisters through the medium of art, which appeals to the eye and the ear."
He has been awarded the first artist's scholarship at the Asian Institute of Liturgy and Music in Manila.
"The Ark of Noah" is a batik work produced for the German churches and reproduced with permission from the Academy of Erzdiozese Bamberg.

Solomon Raj: The Ark of Noah

The Tower of Babylon

They (the people of the world) said, "Now let's build a city with a tower that reaches the sky, so that we can make a name for ourselves and not be scattered all over the earth."
Then the Lord came down to see the city and the tower which those men had built, and he said, "Now then, these are all one people and they speak one language; this is just the beginning of what they are going to do. Soon they will be able to do anything they want! Let us go down and mix up their language so that they will not understand each other." So the Lord scattered them all over the earth, and they stopped building the city.
The city was called Babylon. (Genesis 11: 4-9a)

"Babel is a story of fall and judgement. The people want to be like God. They want to build a city for themselves. They are united, but their unity is only a strategy - unity for security, not for community. They have gathered together only because they do not want to be 'scattered abroad'.
Babel is also the story of God's judgement on human technology, for the people had achieved a high level of culture. It is a judgement on Star Wars, on the sophisticated defence systems and security states of the modern world.
So the Lord comes down and confuses their language. Breakdown in communication will now be a permanent feature of human life."

- T.K. Thomas, India

Like many contemporary artists, Takako Horino of Japan is angered at the distorted sense of values in modern society. In her search for an explanation she has turned to the Old Testament and concentrated on the implications of three stories: the ark of Noah, the tower of Babel and the destruction of Sodom. Each of them is an expression of God's wrath against human stupidity.
In 1987, she completed three series of works which used these Biblical stories as a commentary on modern times.
The tower of Babel compares government fixation with scientific development and weapons of war with its neglect of the people's welfare. The monolith of the tower and its missiles stands in stark contrast to the broken buildings, churches and institutions below.
In the end, all is destroyed. No life exists. A solitary skeleton sitting in front of a television monitor marks the final symbol of humanity's self-destruction.

Takako Horino was born in 1931 in Tokyo. When her home was destroyed by bombing during World War II she moved to Sapporo, Hokkaido and three years later was baptised a Christian.
In 1956 she opened a small stationery shop in Tokyo and began studies at the Musashino College where she specialised in etching and print work. Her work is marked by sensitivity and a delicate touch.
Among many works of contemporary social comment, she has recently completed three series of etchings which portray God's wrath against humankind in the Old Testament.
The Tower of Babel (opposite) is one of these.

Takako Horino: Tower of Babel

Hagar the Slave Girl

Sarai treated Hagar so cruelly that she ran away. The angel of the Lord met Hagar at a spring in the desert on the road to Shur and said, "Hagar, slave of Sarai, where have you come from and where are you going?"
She answered, "I am running away from my mistress."
He said, "Go back to her and be her slave." Then he said, "I will give you so many descendents that no one will be able to count them. You are going to have a son, and you will name him Ishmael, because the Lord has heard your cry of distress." (Genesis 16: 6b-11)

Abraham and Sarah are honoured as the founders of the nation of Israel. Abraham's trust in God to lead him out of Babylon and his willingness to sacrifice his own son are quoted as signs of his great faith. But because Abraham and Sarah were people of wealth and privilege most Asian Christians have difficulty identifying with them. In recent years, many Asians have rediscovered Hagar as a person with whom they can have genuine empathy.
Frank Wesley's moving painting shows Hagar alone in the wilderness. She is prepared to die when the angel meets her. In the midst of hopelessness, God reveals to her that her son Ishmael will be the father of a great nation.

"In the story of Hagar, God clearly shows himself to be the protector of the oppressed and exploited. Hagar's humanity is affirmed. God promises that her son will be the leader of a great nation. The God of Hagar is for all people, not only the chosen ones. He is the God of hope and salvation.
This should humble us a lot. We often have many unwarranted assumptions about ourselves, being privileged for one reason or another. It should be clear to us that God works through other people. It is evident that God is active in lifting up the oppressed and asserting the right of dispossessed persons like Hagar and Ishmael."   - George Ninan, India

Frank Wesley is a fifth generation Indian Christian born in 1923 in Azamgarh, Uttar Pradesh, India. He comes from a long line of artists. His father was a noted singer and violinist.
Wesley studied art in Lucknow where his Hindu professor inspired him not only in his art but also in an appreciation of Jesus Christ and his teaching. After World War II, he studied Japanese art for five years in Kyoto Art University, Japan. He studied two years in the Art Institute of Chicago before returning to India. His paintings have won many awards and he had the distinction of designing the first UNICEF Christmas card: "The Blue Madonna" in 1947. Wesley paints with meticulous attention to detail and technique and his use of background symbolism is a particular feature of his work. He is now retired and living in Queensland, Australia.
Hagar (opposite) was painted in water colour on paper and is in a private collection in Bangalore, India. The colour washes have been manipulated with a pallette knife on rough paper to emphasise the hard rocks which symbolise Hagar's life as a bond-maid.

Frank Wesley: Hagar

The Offering of Isaac

God tested Abraham; he called to him, "Abraham!" And Abraham answered, "Yes, here I am!"
"Take your son," God said, "your only son, Isaac, whom you love so much, and go to the land of Moriah. There on a mountain that I will show you, offer him as a sacrifice to me." Early the next morning Abraham cut some wood for the sacrifice, loaded his donkey, and took Isaac and two servants with him...
But the angel of the Lord called to him from heaven, "Abraham, Abraham!"
He answered, "Yes, here I am."
"Don't hurt the boy or do anything to him," he said. "Now I know that you fear God, because you have not kept back your only son from him." (Genesis: 22: 1-3b, 11,12)

"Isaac was about to be the victim for the burnt-offering. He was to be the sacrificial lamb at the decisive sacrifical act for justice and shalom (reconciliation) between God and God's people, and among the people. His parents, Abraham and Sarah, offered their son as the sacrificial lamb for justice and shalom. They are the faithful ones.
The Christian community believed that Isaac foreshadowed Christ the victim. The victims today are the oppressed and exploited people (the Minjung). Their sacrifice undergirds the life of all people, especially the rich; and their sacrifice sustains humanity. They are the lambs of peace.
Mothers and fathers of the Minjung offer their sons and daughters for production (workers), security (soldiers), and welfare (home-makers) to sustain the community, society and the world. The sacrifice of their children makes them the Isaacs of today.
Korean victims of the A-bomb are Isaacs in the burning of an atomic exploitation, who may bring the seed of peace to bud on earth. Victims of hunger and poverty may force God to bring blessings to the world where the people will be like stars in the sky or sand on the seashore.
Political refugees are sacrificial victims. War widows and orphans, victims of the Korean war, may be the Isaacs of liberation, peace and reunification in the Korean peninsula.
Where is the God who has stopped the killing of Isaac of yesterday and the Isaacs of today? Is God still to come? With all these questions, the mothers and fathers of the Minjung still believe that God will bless them with justice and peace on earth. They are the mothers and fathers of the faithful."

— Kim Yong-Bock, Korea

He Huibing *in one of a number of younger Christian women in China who are building on Chinese traditional art to make new and contemporary statements about the Christian faith.*
A student of He Qi at Nanking she has subsequently joined the staff of the seminary.
Her brush painting of the offering of Isaac is a recent work.

耶和華
以勒

創世記廿三章

一九八二年慧冰畫於金陵

He Huibing: The Sacrifice of Isaac

Isaac and Jacob

(Thinking he was Esau, Isaac blessed Jacob saying) "May God give you dew from heaven and make your fields fertile! May he give you plenty of grain and wine! May nations be your servants, and may peoples bow down before you. May you rule over all your relatives, and may your mother's descendents bow down before you. May those who curse you be cursed, and may those who bless you be blessed." (Genesis 27: 28,29)

"What strikes us most in the story of Jacob is the great distance between his most ambiguous act and God's plans. What could be more ambiguous than Jacob's act of cunning and deception? Not only his crude and simple-minded brother Esau but also his blind, old father, were victims of his criminal act. How could such a morally and religiously monstrous deed have anything to do with God's plans? The gap between them seems insurmountable. But they do become related... It is a theological act of God's saving love for Israel that enabled Old Testament writers to perceive redemptive relationships between the ambiguous human act of Jacob and God's plans.

History, personal or collective, is in one sense a sum total of ambiguous human acts. If this was true in the case of Jacob and Israel, it can also be true for each and every Asian and for the history of our own countries - the history of the Philippines, the history of India, the history of Indochina. We cannot put these ambiguous human histories aside. To remove them is to remove our own history. Until recently, under the influence of traditional theology, we tried to put them aside. We did not know what to do with ourselves as Asians. We could not regard our own history as having some internal relationship with God's plans. Our context is there, but we lose it. We ourselves are the context, but we negate it. Yet, if even Jacob's most ambiguous human act did get incorporated into God's plans, then what about ambiguous Asian selves and ambiguous Asian histories? Ours is the task of incorporating ourselves and the history of our lands into God's plans. God's saving love enables us to go about this task."

-C.S. Song, Taiwan

Masaru Horie was born in Kobe, Japan in 1913. A graduate from the Education Department of Kobe University, he subsequently taught at a primary school in Kobe.
His strong art soon attracted national attention. In 1979 he won the prize of the Ministry of Education and the Yasui Prize in 1980.
He has retained a strong commitment to the church, teaches in Sunday School each week and is a regular contributor to the Japan Christian Artists' Association annual exhibition.
A member of the Japan Watercolour Artists' Association.
His watercolour painting of Isaac and Jacob is in the collection of the Awaji Island Museum.

Masaru Horie: Isaac and Jacob

The Wilderness at Sinai

One day while Moses was taking care of the sheep and goats of his father-in-law Jethro, the priest of Midian, he led the flock across the desert and came to Sinai, the holy mountain. (Exodus 3: 1)

The wilderness experience of the Israelites was the source of their faith - the certainty that they were a chosen people.

"The image of the wilderness holds for many a powerful, unconscious appeal. In a world in which all progress has been thought of only in terms of cultivating and converting the wilderness into something productive and useful to human community, the original undomesticated wilderness stands as a challenge to our rational and intellectual pride. The wilderness is all that we cannot control in nature; it provides the limits to our conscious understanding of the world in which we live and our belief in human order. A call to the wilderness is also linked to our profound attraction to the unconscious. The wilderness is not just something outside our minds, but it is also the unexplored country of our own inner worlds... The wilderness is something we fear but also long for. It stands for the destruction of civilization, but also for the possibility of new sources of wisdom and inspiration. Those who go into the wilderness have to face their own finitude and, in some mysterious way, the spirit of God...

The image of the wilderness has become increasingly important. The voice of the wilderness is the voice of the genuine alternative - something new, something which breaks into the void and meets individuals and nations here and now in the crisis of the present. It is also the voice of the earth, labouring, tortured, seeking a new people to inherit its goodness. Ultimately it is the voice of creation, and by extension, the voice of the artist.

True creativity implies a process of dying, of shedding selfish concern for "me" and "mine", and offering the fruits of one's work as a sacrifice for the good of all creation. All faith systems believe in the creative force of this act of sacrifice. In Indian thought the fire of sacrifice is the recreative energy which establishes all the worlds. It is our human task to keep this fire burning."
                                                    - Jyoti Sahi, India

Chang Ching is a Taiwanese Christian who has perfected the traditional art of wood-carving and used it to illustrate Biblical stories. The size of his works can be guaged from "The Wilderness" (opposite) which captures the sense of isolation and drama in the wilderness wanderings of the Israelites.

Chang Ching: The Wilderness

The Call of Moses

(At Sinai) the angel of the Lord appeared to him as a flame coming from the middle of a bush. Moses saw that the bush was on fire but that it was not burning up. "This is strange," he thought. "Why isn't the bush burning up? I will go closer and see."
When the Lord saw that Moses was coming closer, he called to him from the middle of the bush and said, "Moses! Moses!"
He answered, "Yes, here I am."
God said, "Do not come any closer. Take off your sandals, because you are standing on holy ground. I am the God of your ancestors, the God of Abraham, Isaac, and Jacob." So Moses covered his face, because he was afraid to look at God. (Exodus 3: 2-6)

In verse five Moses is told: "Take off your sandals, because you are standing on holy ground."
You may know that in Korea and Japan we always take off our shoes as we enter homes. The home is a place where people live, but shoes bring in dirt. So we leave that dirt behind and enter cleanly into the home. It shows respect for the people we are visiting. This verse has a lesson for us today. It means that there is a sacred place in which we stand in awe and one that deserves our respect. In today's society that sense of awe has been lost. Today, we think we know it all! There is nothing left to wonder at. And there is no fear of anything. Some play with nuclear weapons as though they were toys, others pollute the environment without knowing the consequences. When people lose their fear of the fearful, then they begin to destroy themselves. When people stop fearing God, they make God a tool for their own purposes. Look at South Africa where the white minority uses God to justify apartheid and injustice. We have to listen carefully to what God says through the other side. That means everyone has to stand under God's judgement. We have to be afraid of that judgement.
When God told Moses to remove his shoes, he was teaching that he, God, was in control. And he is teaching us the same thing. We cannot use God as we please. He is the one who deserves our awe and respect.

            - Lee In-ha, Japan

Paul Koli is Professor of the Print Making Class of the Sir J.J. School of Art, Bombay. He has participated in a number of print-making seminars and in April 1989 studied Japanese print-making in Kyoto with a scholarship from the Asian Christian Art Association.
He is one of the active supporters of the Indian Christian Art Association and has exhibited his religious art widely at churches and church conferences.
His print "Burning Bush" was produced in 1984 and was part of a collection of Christian art which travelled through Europe and America in 1988/89. It shows a strong command of colour in printing.

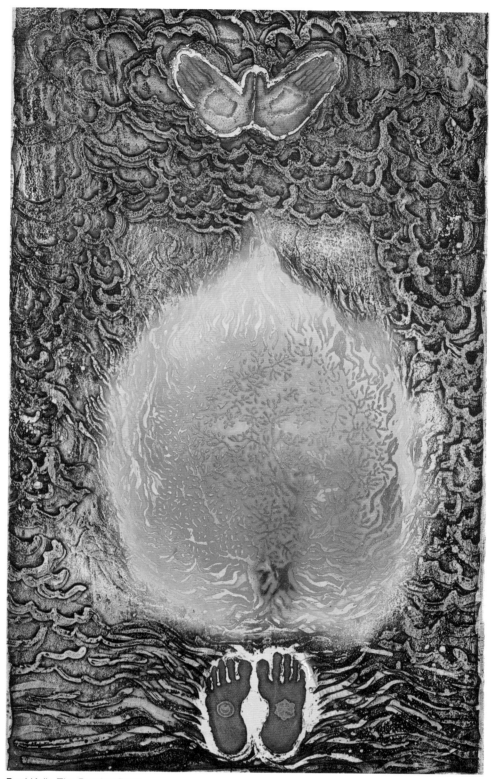

Paul Koli: The Burning Bush

Exodus

The Israelites walked through the sea on dry ground. But when the Egyptian chariots with their horses and drivers went into the sea, the Lord brought the water back, and it covered them. The prophet Miriam, Aaron's sister, took her tambourine, and all the women followed her, playing tambourines and dancing. Miriam sang for them:

"Sing to the Lord, because he has won a glorious victory;
he has thrown the horses and their riders into the sea." (Exodus 15: 19-21)

    In vibrant celebration
        women dance
        waters dance
    celebrating
        community in sisterhood
        solidarity in liberation

    Water is Life
    women birth Life
        Let us celebrate Life
        God's gift of liberation!
                    - Ranjini Rebera, Australia

Dr Sang-Chul Lee became Moderator of the United Church of Canada in 1988. A refugee, imprisoned, tortured, yet a fierce fighter for human rights, he described his conversion in a recent biography:
"After reading the gospels, I tried Paul's letters, but I could make little sense of them. Then I decided to try some of the earlier parts of the Bible and discovered the amazing world of the Old Testament.
The story of Moses was a revelation. The children of Israel suffering under the unjust oppression of Egypt seemed exactly like the Koreans under the Japanese. The story echoed in me. Sometimes I could not sleep. I had to read it over and over again. The God described in these passages did not try to get the better of mortals, like the gods my parents had tried to appease. This God helped people in their struggle. He liberated them. Perhaps he could do the same for all of us.
The Christian God seemed always to change history. This meant that tomorrow things do not have to be as they are today. What is more, this Christian Bible seemed to value people without regard to their origins or social status. It placed a value on the poor, the sick, the downtrodden, the defeated. A man cruelly executed as a criminal gets called the Son of God. It was an utterly crazy concept. But I liked it."

Lucy D'Souza is an active artist living in Bangalore, India.
Her painting of Miriam dancing at the river is one of a series of "Biblical Women" reproduced as the 1990 Lenten veil of Misereor, Germany. Miriam, the prophetess and sister of Moses and Aaron, celebrated the liberation of her people from their Egyptian oppressors. Her dance was supported by other women who joined with her in an act of celebration.
Writing of the story the artist adds that "water is a predominant element in the scene reminding us also of the physical hardship facing women in India as they often have to walk many miles for a pot of water."

Lucy D'Souza: Miriam - Prophetess and Sister

Gideon

Gideon took the men down to the water, and the Lord said to him, "Separate everyone who laps up the water with his tongue like a dog, from everyone who gets down on his knees to drink." There were three hundred men who scooped up water in their hands and lapped it; all the others got down on their knees to drink. The Lord said to Gideon, "I will rescue you and give you victory over the Midianites with the three hundred men who lapped the water. Tell everyone else to go home." (Judges 7: 5-7)

Faith without common sense achieves little.

Ten thousand soldiers of Gideon volunteered to fight the Midianites and had the belief that God would protect them, but when they were told to drink from the stream most of them put their face right into the water, a stupid thing to do for people who were expecting an enemy attack.

God's word to Gideon was that he was willing to achieve with 300 sensible followers what would have been difficult with 10,000 thoughtless ones.

A good soldier is not violent.
A good fighter is not angry.
A good winner is not vengeful.
A good employer is humble.
This is known as the virtue of not striving.
This is known as the ability to work
   with people.
This, since ancient times, has been known as
the ultimate unity with heaven.
      - Tao te Ching, 6th Century B.C.

Ryohei Koiso grew up as an active member of the Kobe church and had a strong ambition to be a painter. Although his family opposed this course his grandmother said, "If you are going to be a painter, you should make it your life's ministry."

After study in Europe Koiso returned to Tokyo and in 1959 become a professor at Tokyo Art College. His Christian art works provided the illustrations for the Revised Version of the Bible in colloquial Japanese.

A popular and distinguished Japanese artist, he died in 1988 at the age of 85.

His illustration of Gideon's men at the river shows the research and planning which went into all his works. The painting is produced with a bamboo drawing nib and Chinese ink with a light wash of colour.

Ryohei Koiso: Gideon

The Song of Ruth

Naomi said to her, "Ruth, your sister-in-law has gone back to her people and to her god. Go back home with her."

But Ruth answered, "Don't ask me to leave you! Let me go with you. Wherever you go, I will go; wherever you live, I will live. Your people will be my people, and your God will be my God. Wherever you die, I will die, and that is where I will be buried. May the Lord's worst punishment come upon me if I let anything but death separate me from you!" (Ruth 1: 15-17)

"Ruth's great love for Naomi - her Jewish mother-in-law, enables her to dedicate her young life to protect and support her. Naomi, herself a widow, was not so keen to go back to Bethlehem with a widowed daughter-in-law who belonged to another race. But Ruth embraced and clung to her...There was nothing in Ruth's mind which could come between her and Naomi - least of all racial differences. She was totally committed to 'the other' in Naomi.

Ruth's self-less devotion to her mother-in-law challenges Boaz to a similar response - he takes them both under his wing. On the occasion of the birth of Boaz and Ruth's son, Obed, the women of Jerusalem, too, find themselves overcoming their racist prejudices in acclaiming Ruth the Moabitess as "being better than seven sons.'"

— Chitra Fernando, Sri Lanka

Ruth and Naomi

Yoshihei Miya was born in Japan in 1893 in the Niigata Prefecture. He studied in Tokyo Academy and taught in Suwa Girl's High School. In 1966 he visited the Holy Land and his book of art and poetry from that trip became popular in Japan. He died in 1971 in Kyoto.

Yoshihei Miya: Ruth and Naomi (Detail)

Saul and David

The next day an evil spirit from God suddenly took control of Saul, and he raved in his house like a madman. David was playing the harp, as he did every day, and Saul was holding a spear. "I'll pin him to the wall," Saul said to himself, and he threw the spear at him twice; but David dodged each time. (1 Samuel 18: 10,11)

Medieval and renaissance artists delighted in sculpting or painting David. Statues of him by Donatello, Michaelangelo and Bernini show him as the young giant killer. Titian and Caravaggio painted him as the muscular young victor.

He Qi has ignored these triumphalist images and turned instead to the dramatic and human conflict between King Saul and his young protege David. When Saul throws the spear at David while he is playing a harp it exposes all the complex psychological relationships of jealousy, anger and paranoia present in the story.

The control of anger and violence in society has become a lively issue in every country. The Doctrines of Buddha (Dhammapada) offer some sensible advice on anger:

> Leave anger and forsake pride and you will be
>   free from all bondage.
> Do not seek status and position, call nothing
> your own and you will be free from suffering.
> Keep your anger under control and you will be
> able to drive a rolling chariot. If not you will
>   just be holding the reins.
> Overcome anger by love and evil by good.
> Overcome greed by generosity, lies by truth.
>   Three steps take you closer to god:
>   Speak the truth,
>   Do not yield to anger,
>   Give to those who ask.

He Qi is the Art Instructor at Nanjing Theological Seminary, China. His work is a further illustration of the importance the Chinese church places on the role of art in the church.

He Qi's work first came to the attention of people outside China through his use of paper-cuts to illustrate the Biblical message. These finely cut papers have been used to provide graphic illustrations for many publications.

He has stressed the importance of developing Chinese indigenous art and writes: "People's aesthetic sense has begun to enter a multidimensional period. In art, the people desire change, not stagnation; they want variety, not uniformity. Each country and each people should have its own artistic style and distinctive features. The more indigenous art is, the more international it will be... A solitary flower is not spring; spring is spring because there is a riot of flowers."

He Qi visited Japan in 1990 to study the influence of Christian art in that country.

He Qi: Saul and David

Elijah and the Ravens

Then the Lord said to Elijah, "Leave this place and go east and hide yourself near Cherith Brook, east of the Jordan. The brook will supply you with water to drink, and I have commanded ravens to bring you food there."
Elijah obeyed the Lord's command, and went and stayed by Cherith Brook. He drank water from the brook, and ravens brought him bread and meat every morning and every evening.

(1 Kings 17: 2-6)

Elijahs's anguish over his country and the rule of King Ahab became an increasingly heavy burden to carry. He fled the city for the wilderness and there found that God provided for his needs.

> Take thou the burden, Lord;
> I am exhausted with this heavy load.
> My tired hands tremble,
> And I stumble, stumble
> Along the way.
> Oh, lead with thine unfailing arm
> Again today.
>
> Unless thou lead me, Lord
> The road I journey on is all too hard.
> Through trust in thee alone
> Can I go on.
>
> Yet not for self alone
> Thus do I groan;
> My people's sorrows are the load I bear.
> Lord, hear my prayer -
> May thy strong hand
> Strike off all chains
> That load my well-loved land
> God, draw her close to thee.
>
> - Toyohiko Kagawa, Japan

Osamu Nishizaka was born in Japan, September 1911. His father, who was a publisher of Christian Education materials, had considerable influence on his life and encouraged him to take up a life of art. His membership in the United Church of Christ in Japan led him to focus much of his art on religious themes.
Nishizaka is a member of the Kodo Art Association.

Osamu Nishizaka: Elijah and the Ravens

Elijah on Mt Horeb

"Go out and stand before me on top of the mountain," the Lord said to him (Elijah). Then the Lord passed by and sent a furious wind that split the hills and shattered the rocks - but the Lord was not in the wind. The wind stopped blowing, and then there was an earthquake - but the Lord was not in the earthquake. After the earthquake there was a fire - but the Lord was not in the fire. And after the fire there was the soft whisper of a voice.

When Elijah heard it, he covered his face with his cloak and went out and stood at the entrance of the cave. (1 Kings 19: 11-13a)

After Elijah the prophet had exposed the false prophets, Queen Jezebel tried to kill him but he escaped to Mt Horeb.

"No wonder Elijah was afraid and fled for his life. He was a man of courage, but what good is courage if it is not sustained by the encouragement of others? There is only so much that people can take.

Life doesn't have much meaning when you are completely cut off from others. When you have struggled and thought you have succeeded - only to come up against people's fickleness and the hatred of those whose power you have thwarted...

After food, drink and a rest and some time on the holy mountain, there is this question: Is this the place you should be, where you want to do my work?

Elijah states his case. 'I have always served you - you alone.' Nothing could make his loyalty swerve.

In the Muslim creed, *La ilaha 'ila Allah*, we find a similar devotion - 'There is no God but Allah.' Anybody, indeed anything, that comes between the believer and Allah (Which, by the way, is the word used by Christians in Indonesia and elsewhere for 'God') is an idol. The true believer should serve God alone.

What answer is there to Elijah's tale of woe? God revealing God's self to the utterly disillusioned Elijah. But God was not in the 'furious wind' nor in the earthquake, nor in the fire. God was in the 'soft whisper of a voice'.

It is in the ordinary course of daily life that God speaks to us to give us God's directions. 'Sure as the sunrise and fresh as the morning' (Lamentations) God is in our life. God is not a remote deity floating beyond our reach somewhere up there, but God is personally accessible and intelligible to us in the framework of our experience."

- Marianne Katoppo, Indonesia

Sister Genevieve of Bangalore has been described by Dr Richard Taylor as "the only foreigner I take seriously as an Indian Christian artist." Born in France, she has given her life to India. A skilled artist, Genevieve sees painting in an Indian style as a way of entry into Hindu homes.

Together with Sister Claire (see page 170) she was commissioned by the Catholic church to paint a series of posters on the Bible for use in Christian education. This mammoth task meant the two Sisters had to paint a total of 140 art works in the space of two years.

As will be seen from "Elijah on Mt Horeb" the posters were works of art in their own right. Painted in water colours and reproduced by the Bangalore catechetical centre, they have influenced masses of young Indian Christians and enabled them to see Christianity in their own idiom.

Sister Genevieve: A Still, Small Voice

Job

When the day came for the heavenly beings to appear before the Lord, Satan was there among them. The Lord asked him, "What have you been doing?"
Satan answered, "I have been walking here and there, roaming around the earth."
"Did you notice my servant Job?" the Lord asked. "There is no one on earth as faithful and good as he is. He worships me and is careful not to do anything evil."
Satan replied, "Would Job worship you if he got nothing out of it? You have always protected him and his family and everything he owns. You bless everything he does, and you have given him enough cattle to fill the whole country. But now suppose you take away everything he has - he will curse you to your face!" (Job 1:6-11)

"In Hinduism, suffering is treated as an inalienable part of life. Suffering is seen to be the result of *karma* and is understood to be governed by the inexorable law of *karma samsara*. Here physical and even "social" suffering is related to man's moral and ethical life. Suffering becomes a subject for religious reflection and action. In and through suffering the soul grows in knowledge, maturity and experience all of which helps the final emancipation of the soul.
Equally important is the Buddhist understanding of suffering as *dukka*. Here the whole of existence is understood in terms of suffering: to be is to suffer, and the prime aim is to work for the cessation of the process of life itself which brings with it the universal experience of suffering.
There is also in Asia an increasing number of people who tend to limit their analysis of suffering within the ideological presuppositions based on economic realities.
Christians have often claimed to have the answers for most expressions of suffering. Often one hears sermons from Luke 4 on 'good tidings to the poor', 'set at liberty those that are oppressed', 'sight to the blind' etc., and the claim that the Christian message effectively deals with the problem of social suffering. The gospel message is projected as the answer to the discriminating and dehumanizing tendencies in society and Christ as the answer to the meaninglessness of existence. The cross and resurrection are seen as providing in some sense the answer to suffering. We must, however, move away from generalizations and from theorising to ask very basic questions. For it is evident in history that the church has not proved to be the answer to the various forms of suffering and hope."

- Wesley Ariarajah, Sri Lanka

Goro Kakei of Japan sculpts in a dramatic and forceful style which halts us and makes us reflect on life. The Japanese poet, Asao Shima, wrote of his work, "When I encounter the work of Goro Kakei, I experience a profound silence. From a very practical viewpoint I feel grateful for any kind of experience that submerges us into the depths of silence, even for a minute, in our busy and hectic modern life.
Goro Kakei is a unique artist. He has a passionate purity far away from any gesture of self-promotion. Probably more than anyone else, he is aware of the fact that he is looking up from the deep abyss of this world. From this point of view we can understand his strictness regarding himself and his compassion towards others."
In "Job" Kakei catches the mood of suffering and distress. It was cast in 1961.

Job: Goro Kakei

(Photo: Toura Misawa)

Psalm 1

Happy are those who reject the advice of evil men, who do not follow the example of sinners or join those who have no use for God. Instead, they find joy in obeying the Law of the Lord, and they study it day and night. They are like trees that grow beside a stream, that bear fruit at the right time, and whose leaves do not dry up. They succeed in everything they do.
(Psalm 1:1-3)

The T'ang dynasty (618-907) was the golden age of Chinese art and culture. Painting trees as a separate discipline began at that time and even when China was invaded from the north the arts continued to flourish. The tradition of painting particularly "friendly" trees began at that time. The "three worthy friends in the cold winter" were the pine, the bamboo and the plum blossom.

The plum blossom had a special place in the hearts of the people. This is because it could resist the most severe winter elements. In the worst blizzards the plum trees stand upright and blossom in the cold air. It is such a vivid symbol of strength that the plum blossom was adopted as the national flower of Tai·wan.

Over the centuries, many famous Chinese artists have painted the plum blossom.

Where the mind is without fear and the head is
held high,
where knowledge is free;
where the world has not been broken up into
fragments by narrow domestic walls;
where words come out of the depth of truth;
where tireless striving stretches its arms towards perfection;
where the clear stream of reason has not lost its
way
into the dreary desert sand of dead habit;
where the mind is led forward by thee
into ever-widening thought and action -
into the heaven of freedom, my Father, let my
country awake.
                              - Rabindranath.Tagore, Bengal

K'ou Pei Shen comes from an old family of scholars in Ching Chow, Shantung Province, China. By the age of ten he had learned the four Chinese classics and received formal training in calligraphy.
While studying civil engineering in College he spent much of his spare time sketching. During the Sino-Chinese war he travelled thousands of miles on foot through China to reach Szechuan. He had many adventures, often suffering from lack of food, and has recorded some of these experiences in his paintings. After the war he worked for nearly thirty years in Japan before returning to Taiwan in 1979 where he has had to battle ill health and failing eyesight.During this time he has concentrated on painting plum trees in the traditional Chinese style.

K'ou Pei Shen: Plum Blossom

The Lord is my shepherd;
I have everything I need.
He lets me rest in fields of green grass
and leads me to quiet pools of fresh water. (Psalm 23:1,2)

Chung Lap Kwan turns to the water to seek the meaning of the twenty-third Psalm.

Those who neglect to drink
of the spring of experience
are apt to die of thirst
in the desert of ignorance
- Li Po, China

The presence or absence of water has dominated Asian thought for centuries. The power of the Ganges, the Yangtse and the Mekong to flood the land and bring death and devastation is well documented. In other places, the failure of monsoon rains or long periods of drought can wreak similar havoc for society.

The weakest things in the world can defeat
the strongest things in the world.
Nothing under heaven is more soft and yielding than water, yet for attacking the solid and strong nothing is better and nothing its equal.
Weak can overcome strong
Yielding can overcome stiff
Under heaven, all the world knows this
But nobody puts it into practice.
The wise person says:
The one who accepts the humiliation of the people is fit to rule them,
The man who accepts in his person the country's disasters deserves to be king of the universe.
These are words of truth,
The truth is often spoken in paradox.
- Tao te Ching

Chung Lap Kwan was one of a small group of young Hong Kong artists who began, in 1970, to forge a new style within traditional Chinese ink painting. For twenty years he has persevered with one of the most difficult of all art techniques: water painting.

In this process ink floats on water and by means of hydrocarbon materials (such as gasoline and kerosene) unique effects are created and transmitted onto paper. It is a creative process demanding much discipline and experience. Many copies are made until the final one emerges. "When an aesthetic experience pervades my mind," says Chung, "the spirit of the mountains and the feel of the water are elicited from my inner world and conveyed onto the printing paper." He compares the experience to the birth of a child.

Chung dedicates all his art to God. Brought up in the mountains he has never lost his love for the "spiritual atmosphere of the mountains, and ...life-giving mountain streams." It is easy to see the spirituality underlying his work and to know that his work "The Melody of Water" (opposite) draws inspiration from the twenty-third Psalm.

Chung Lap Kwan: The Melody of Water

As a deer longs for a stream of cool water,
　　　so I long for you, O God.
I thirst for you, the living God.
　　　When can I go and worship in your presence?
Day and night I cry,
　　　and tears are my only food;
all the time my enemies ask me,
　　　"Where is your God?"　　　(Psalm 42:1-3)

"The artist surveys the layout of hills and streams, estimates the width and length of the land, examines the distribution of mountain peaks and observes the airy forlornness of clouds and mists. He looks at the earth spread before him and takes a swift glance at the distant ranges, and knows that they are under the overlordship of heaven and earth. Heaven has the standard to transform the spirit of hills and streams, earth has this norm to activate their pulse beat, and I have this one-stroke (of brush and ink) to penetrate into their very body and spirit."

- Shi-t'ao, China (1641-1720)

"This is the deep insight of a Chinese painter of mountains and waters. The intuitive wisdom of Chinese nature artists tells them that nature is not something alien to human beings, that it is not something standing over against them. We are in nature and nature is in us, and together we and nature are in God...

Shih-t'ao had the 'one-stroke of brush and ink' to penetrate the spirit of what he sees, feels and touches round about him. What sort of 'one-stroke' do theologians have to have in order to penetrate the mystery of God's ways with Asian nations and peoples?

Our 'theological one-stroke' is no other than God's saving love for the world. With this one-stroke of God's saving love, we can learn to paint the landscape of God's work out of the historical, cultural, and religious experiences of the peoples of Asia.

All this should not sound strange to us. For it is with this theological one-stroke that writers of the Old Testament, storytellers, poets, historians, and theologians, wrote the history of Israel."

- C.S.Song, Taiwan

Yang Chien-hou is one of the senior leaders of the Chinese church. Born in 1910 he continues to work as a professor of the Art Department in Nanjing Normal University.
His work has been widely used in the churches. The painting of Psalm 42 was chosen to be one of the works used in the 1984 calendar of the Chinese Christians.

Yang Chien-hou: As the Deer

Psalm 56

When I am afraid, O Lord Almighty,
I put my trust in you. I trust in God and am not afraid;
I praise him for what he has promised. What can a mere human being do to me?...
You know how troubled I am;
You have kept a record of my tears. Aren't they listed in your book?
The day I call to you,
my enemies will be turned back.
I know this: God is on my side - The Lord, whose promises I praise.
In him I trust, and I will not be afraid.   (Psalm 56: 3,4, 8-10)

"We must not forget that there are many people who cannot come to the big evangelistic meetings. I mean those workers labouring hard with beads of sweat; those young boys and girls who are constantly running in the factories; those sick people living in the wood and tar-paper shacks and wondering how to get their next meal; those who are struggling to live with polluted air and water in rural and fishing villages; and those who are poor, enviously watching the luxurious life of the cats and dogs of the rich, despite the fact that they themselves were born as human beings."　　　　　- Park Hyung Kyu, Korea

Prayer! Prayer! Prayer!
May heaven accept this prayer of mine
repeated over and over again for many months.
May the edge of my soul become sharper.
Even if my breast explodes in agonized wailing,
let me set out on this journey.
Let me go out into the wilderness
into the land that nearly drives me mad
with its awakening bitterness.
The land over which stars sparkle
in the frozen winter dawn.
Let me pray alone
let me decide alone:
to be with the people, at the bottom,
to be beaten with them,
to decay with them,
and finally to rise up gallantly from the earth
with them
in the bright morning sunshine,
with our heads held high.
　　　　　　　　- Kim Chi Ha, Korea

Lee Chul-soo *is a young Korean folk artist with no formal training but his powerful work has been described as having "the strength of the burning sun, the simplicity of nature and a kind of humour which cuts like a knife."*
His paintings resemble woodblocks but they are each one-of-a-kind. He draws an outline on oiled paper, normally used for traditional floor heating units (ondoru), then the area around the lines is spread with moist yellow earth. Coal tar is then applied and once it has set, the painting is washed to remove the earth. The lines are sharp and vivid. Lee then adds colour from a cloth-dyeing process he has adapted.
His work has a strong social action orientation but like many Korean Christians, the Biblical message is always close to the surface in his thinking.
His painting of the woman worker is deliberately surrounded by flowers to point to the hope of heaven which sustains her.

Lee Chul-soo: Dream of the Woman Textile Worker

Song of Songs

The winter is over; the rains have stopped;
in the countryside the flowers are in bloom.
This is the time for singing;
the song of doves is heard in the fields.

(Song of Songs 2: 11,12)

Christians in China have a special affection for these verses from the Song of Songs. They reflect not only the change in seasons but also their hope for a better future for all people.

A popular hymn used frequently in China is also based on this text. The Mandarin title is "Dong-tian yi wang, Yu-shui yi zhi" and the translation reads:

Winter has passed, the rain is o'er
     earth is a bloom, songs fill the air.
Linger no more, why must you wait?
     Rise up my love, come follow me.

Refrain:
Jesus, my Lord, my love, my all,
body and soul forever yours,
in dale so dark, I long for you,
abide with me in spring anew.

Wu Kyo-ting *was born in China in 1935.*
He is a teacher at the Jiangsu Provincial Academy of Arts in Nanjing.

Wu Kyo-ting: Song of Songs

The Dream of Peace

He will settle disputes among great nations.
They will hammer their swords into plows
and their spears into pruning knives.
Nations will never again go to war,
never prepare for battle again.

(Isaiah 2:4)

"In Hebrew, the word for peace is *shalom*. Shalom principally involves health and the good life. It is protection by God's favourable promise (Judg. 18:6) or by someone who cares for one's needs (Judg. 19:20). Restoration to health is restoration to peace (Isa. 38:17). The individual's peace is synonymous with the good life, for it involves healthful sleep (Ps. 4:8), length of life (Prov. 3:2) and posterity (Ps. 37:37).

Just as the peace of the individual is his/her health and safety, the peace of the nation, or of the family, or of communal life is its prosperity and security...

Shalom, in other words, is much more than the absence of war or accepting Jesus to one's heart. It is much more than 'inner' serenity, which is how Christians often try to spiritualize it. The Biblical understanding of shalom is materialistic like the questions asked in the last judgment according to Matthew 25:31f...

What this means is that peace is not possible while thousands suffer hunger, little children die of malnutrition, indigenous people are denied land rights, women are denied equality with men, workers are denied the right to strike, human beings are despised and discriminated by human beings on the basis of colour, class or race. Peace is denied in a land where people are tortured and kept in police custody without being given a proper trial... It is to these types of situations that the prophets cried out and spoke of God's judgment and condemnation.

On the other hand there is at least a taste of peace or shalom in any country, society or family where there is a genuine concern for one's neighbour, a commitment to one another and a deep solidarity which expresses itself in the form of sharing and standing in for each other."

— Rienzie Perera, Sri Lanka

Gai Muo-seng was born in China in 1941.
His original painting of World Peace was 192x51 cms and it captures a theme which is of particular interest to churches in China.
The painting was part of the 1984 calendar of the Chinese churches.
He works for the Jiangsu Provincial Art Museum.

他們要將刀打成犁
頭把槍打成鐮刀
戊辰秋益武屬

Gai Muo-seng: World Peace

Like the Eagle

Those who trust in the Lord for help
will find their strength renewed.
They will rise on wings like eagles;
they will run and not get weary;
they will walk and not grow weak.

(Isaiah 40:31)

Lord, Holy Spirit,
You are as the mother eagle with her young,
Holding them in peace under your feathers.
On the highest mountain you have built your nest,
Above the valley, above the storms of the world,
Where no hunter ever comes.

Lord, Holy Spirit,
You are the bright cloud in whom we hide,
In whom we know already that
    the battle has been won.
You bring us to our Brother Jesus
To rest our heads upon his shoulder.

Lord, Holy Spirit,
In the love of friends you are building a new house,
Heaven is with us when you are with us.
You are singing your song in the hearts of the poor.
Guide us, wound us, heal us. Bring us to God.

- James K. Baxter, Aotearoa / New Zealand

Lu Hsu Chia is a Taiwanese artist living in Singapore who began her interest in brush painting after her marriage.
Like many brush painters she enjoys the use of space as part of the composition and prefers a simple, uncluttered picture. Her art is directly related to her Christian faith and many of her works are based on a Biblical text.
Her philosophy on commercial art is simple. "Many people like to make a lot of money and spend it on material goods. I was brought up to believe that money comes from God and goes back to God. Also, I have a deep sense of gratitude at possessing this artistic talent and my reward is the doing of the art. When I received my first scholarship prize, a rather large sum of money, without hesitation I gave it to the church. It seemed right for me to do so."
Her painting of the eagle is based on the reading from Isaiah 40.

Lu Hsu Chia: Mount Up With Wings

The Laws of God

Even storks know when it is time to return; doves, swallows, and thrushes know when it is time to migrate. But, my people, you do not know the laws by which I rule you. (Jeremiah 8:7)

"Birds migrate. They know when to leave and when to return. And they know where to go and how to get there.

Animals hibernate. They know when to stop and how long to rest. They have their season of sabbath. Not as God had it on the seventh day, after completing the work of creation in six days (Genesis 2:2). Hibernation, like migration, is solely for survival.

These are part of nature's order and in that sense part of 'the law of the Lord.' But that law, insofar as it affects animals and birds appears immutable and absolute. It cannot be challenged. The option of disobedience does not exist.

That is why the Lord's complaint is not too convincing, at least on first reading. The birds cannot return to the Lord, because they cannot depart from the Lord. We can depart, and we do most of the time.

There is a similar passage in the first chapter of Isaiah.

> The ox knows its owner,
> and the ass its master's crib;
> but Israel does not know.
> My people does not understand. (1: 3)

That makes a litle more sense. The complaint, in this instance, has a relational context. As the preceding verse makes clear, it is God's own children, reared and brought up with loving care, who have rebelled against God. It is a touchingly human complaint.

That, perhaps, is the point of Jeremiah 8: 7. It is the humanity of God, supremely expressed in Jesus Christ, that makes claim on our humanity. The law is not the same for us as it is for the rest of creation. We can choose to ignore it; the rest of creation cannot. That is both our bane and our glory. And that God allows it is the measure of God's love.

By not choosing to respond to that love we continue to bring pain to God. We also hurt the rest of creation, as we know only too well today when there are fewer birds and fewer places they can migrate to."

- T.K. Thomas, India

Ayako Araki was born in 1913 in North-East China. While pursuing her study at Shoin Women's College she joined the art club and discovered her love of art.

After marriage her husband encouraged her to enter the Kyoto Dokuritsu Art Institute and she became a member of the Dokuritsu Artist's Association in 1967.

She spends hours painting objects such as an old mud wall, birds, insects and the roots of old trees. For her they symbolize the stream of vibrant life.

"Migrating Birds" (opposite), was painted on her first visit to Palestine when she saw the birds migrating and remembered the faithfulness of God's promise in Jeremiah. It is in the collection of the Asian Christian Art Association, Kyoto.

Ayako Araki: Migrating Birds

Opposite:
The Last Supper
by Sadao Watanabe, Japan

SADAO WATANABE 1982

The New Testament

The Announcement

The angel said to her, "Don't be afraid, Mary; God has been gracious to you. You will become pregnant and give birth to a son, and you will name him Jesus."...
Mary said to the angel, "I am a virgin. How, then, can this be?"
The angel answered, "The Holy Spirit will come on you, and God's power will rest upon you. For this reason the holy child will be called the Son of God."...
"I am the Lord's servant," said Mary; "may it happen to me as you have said." And the angel left her. (Luke 1: 30,31;34,35,38)

When the Asian Christian Art Association held a conference on the theme of the Magnificat, Alphonso began to reflect on the experiences of the young woman, Mary. In a series of several paintings, he showed her at the moment of her visitation.
He saw Mary listening to the message with her body slightly twisted as if in an Indian dance. The spirit comes to her as an egg - the symbol of fertility, or a flower or a dove.
In the large painting (opposite), the message, decorated with a white flower, is about to enter her body. At the time Mary is looking at a lamp whose light has been extinguished. The green background symbolises life and hope.

Annunciation

Alphonso is a South Indian artist born in Bangalore in 1940. Though deeply steeped in traditional Hindu religion he was encouraged by missionaries to paint for the church and began to explore the life of Christ in depth. He says, "No other religious master has been so personal, so communicative and so loveable as Christ, ready to lay down his entire life in fulfilling the needs of society. He has been a suffering symbol for painters for centuries."
Alphonso believes Christ visited India to explore their religious traditions and he painted a series of works on Christ in Benares and in Mathura. "I have always thought of Christ as a person of Eastern origin," he says.
Alphonso teaches art at the Madras College of Art and Crafts. He paints in oil on canvas.

Alphonso: Annunciation

The Birth of Jesus

While they were in Bethlehem, the time came for her to have her baby. She gave birth to her first son, wrapped him in strips of cloth and laid him in a manger - there was no room for them to stay in the inn. (Luke 2: 6,7)

Even in Asia, Christmas is universally celebrated as a time of giving and family gatherings. In poor squatter areas of the Philippines the season has an air of joy and celebration.
Shirley Murray of Aotearoa/New Zealand caught some of the special meaning of Christmas for the poor in a carol. The music, written by I-to Loh of Taiwan, is called "Smokey Mountain" an allusion to the huge rubbish dump in Manila, Philippines, where hundreds of poor people scratch in the trash for food.

Born among the poor on a stable floor,
cold and raw, you know our hunger,
weep our tears and share our anger
yet you tell us more, born among the poor.

Every child needs bread till the world is fed:
you give bread, your hands enable,
all to gather round one table
Christmas must be shared, every child
needs bread.

Son of poverty shame us till we see
self-concerned, how we deny you
by our greed we crucify you
on a Christmas tree, son of poverty.

Le Van Dai came to Hong Kong as a refugee from Vietnam in 1984 and was placed in the Kai Tak refugee camp. In his homeland he had been educated at an Art Academy in Saigon and became a practising artist so when he entered the refugee camp he began to take classes in art with the younger children.
He painted the nativity (opposite) for Steven Neisham, a Lutheran missionary who was assisting the refugees. It is painted on dark-coloured paper using water-based paints. In the picture Mary is dressed in traditional tribal clothing and the motif is continued through the background.
Le Van Dai was granted political asylum in Australia.

Le Van Dai: Nativity

The Nativity

Suddenly a great army of heaven's angels appeared with the angel, singing praises to God:
"Glory to God in the highest heaven,
and peace on earth to those with whom he is pleased!" (Luke 2: 13,14)

When Yasuo Ueno was a young child he returned home from a Sunday School party and suddenly remembered that the gift from his Sunday School teacher had been left at the church. His mother took him back and they searched everywhere but without success. The child was heart-broken.

The next day the teacher came to the house and told them he had found the gift near the foyer of the church. Ueno examined the parcel and noticed that it was wrapped as before but the ribbon was different! He writes:

"Even now, after so many years, that gift, a book of Bible pictures, is one of my treasures. For many years I have wanted to paint the Christmas story. Once begun I thought of that Christmas day - of myself and my teacher, and his care and concern for this unhappy child, and his replacing the lost book. Now, more than 30 years later, if I could somehow present my book, *The First Christmas* to him, I would indeed be grateful."

The First Christmas

Yasuo Ueno was born in Japan in 1926 and is a graduate of the Tokyo Art Academy.
Currently, he is a professor of Tamma Art College in Tokyo, Japan. He has travelled widely in Europe and Asia and much of his art reflects the influences of these visits. The gilding of orthodox icons is reflected in some of his works. He gives great attention to the framing of his paintings.
He has received many awards in Japan and exhibited by invitation at the Japanese International Art Exhibition and the Japanese Mobile Art Exhibition.
The paintings shown here are from his book "Saisho no Kurisumasu" (The First Christmas). The works are painted in natural pigments on silk. (Publishers: Shiko-Sha Co, Tokyo)

Yasuo Ueno: A Multitude of the Heavenly Host

The Song of Mary

Mary said, "My heart praises the Lord;
>   my soul is glad because of God my Saviour,
>   for he has remembered me, his lowly servant!
From now on all people will call me happy,
>   because of the great things the Mighty God has done for me.
His name is holy;
>   from one generation to another he shows mercy to those who honour him.
He has stretched out his mighty arm
>   and scattered the proud with all their plans.
He has brought down mighty kings from their thrones, and lifted up the lowly.
He has filled the hungry with good things,
>   and sent the rich away with empty hands." (Luke 1: 46-53)

"Thinking of Mary, I do not exalt in her supposed purity, for that is too narrow a perspective which does her no justice. I see her in the wider context of love and self-giving. I admire and appreciate her sensitivity to social injustices and her readiness to take moral risks for the sake of a needed social change. That is on one level. On another level, I see Mary as the pre-eminent model of humanity, growing into the full image of God. As the receptive virgin (receptive to the action of God) and the creative mother (sharing the mission of bringing the good news of salvation to the world), she is the model, not only for woman, but also for man. She is the new human being (man-woman) receptive before God who calls her/him to be the Imago Dei.

Human liberation often seems to be a grim and joyless struggle. The Magnificat shows otherwise. And I exult in the fact that this Asian woman, this Mary, upon her encounter with God bursts out into this great song of thanksgiving and joy given to God, who liberates through the oppressed themselves. Through Mary, women in some special way personify the oppressed, although she represents all oppressed people, not just women.

Mary is the truly liberated, fully liberated human being - compassionate and free."

- Marianne Katoppo, Indonesia

Wang Hon-yi was born in China in 1942. He is a professional artist painting in the nanga (Chinese brush-painting) style.
His Christmas painting in 1984 was used by the Chinese church in its annual calendar.
He works for the Jiangsu Provincial Art Museum.

我的心靈要穩妥
好象斷過奶的孩子
在他母親的懷中
壬戌年鴻儀畫

Wang Hon-yi: Safe in His Mother's Arms

Mary

When Joseph and Mary had finished doing all that was required by the law of the Lord, they returned to their home town of Nazareth in Galilee. The child grew and became strong; he was full of wisdom, and God's blessings were upon him. (Luke 2:39,40)

"Mary is truly with us in the Philippines and we see her face reflected in the faces of so many of our women who are undergoing the same pain and suffering that she herself endured. Mary knew poverty and deprivation. In Bethlehem she and Joseph had no money to pay for a room so they could find no decent place in which to stay. Their powerlessness is so like the situation of the women and children of the slums... How many mothers from Argentina to South Korea, from Turkey to South Africa, from Chile to the Philippines, are sharing Mary's harrowing ordeal?... Today, Mary stands with all the women in the world who are poor, deprived and oppressed, offering her own solidarity.

Mary is truly our mother and definitely our closest ally. She is one with us in our suffering and in our struggle...

Despite the sufferings and misery of our people today, there will be the dawning of a new heaven and a new earth. The poor who are faithful to the Gospel will enter the kingdom and experience, with Mary, all the joy and glory of a just and humane society.

This promise encourages us to face the present risks. It gives us hope to defeat our fears and sense of hopelessness. Our discipleship and servanthood bring us to a humble acceptance of the same pain and anguish which Mary accepted so willingly as part of her own mission. Knowing Mary's love for her children, we believe that one day we shall overcome and we will see the kingdom."

— Karl Gaspar, Philippines

Carlos Francisco has a special place in Philippine art. A gifted painter, he rediscovered the art of mural painting in the Philippines and for thirty years created the majestic works which now mark many of Manila's civic buildings. He was deeply steeped in Philippine life and never left the country to travel. He died during Holy Week, 1969 at the age of 57 and was honoured throughout the country as a national treasure. No painter of his time was more attuned to the spirit of the land and people.

The first published collection of his works was in 1985 through the good offices of the Asian Christian Art Association and the Kajima Foundation for the Art in Japan. His "Madonna of the Bamboo" painted in 1962 (oil on wood) captures the sweeping lines of the dress of a Philippine peasant girl and is a fitting celebration of the young mother Mary.

Carlos Francisco: Madonna of the Bamboo

The Flight into Egypt

An angel of the Lord appeared in a dream to Joseph and said, "Herod will be looking for the child in order to kill him. So get up, take the child and his mother and escape to Egypt, and stay there until I tell you to leave."
Joseph got up, took the child and his mother, and left during the night for Egypt, where he stayed until Herod died. (Matthew 2: 13b-15a)

There in the midst of darkness
They made their journey,
The journey that was the first
For the one born but a short time ago.

It was a cold, uncertain journey
With few possessions.
There would be no friends
To welcome them to Egypt.

The sky continuously dark:
No sign that dawn was coming,
Yet hope they had in the little one
Peaceful in the arms of Mary.

Here is the longed for promise,
Immanuel - God with us.
Darkness may still prevail
But we know it is encompassed by light.
                    - Masao Takenaka, Japan

Two thousand years have slipped by
like freshlets in the Ganges
since St Thomas came to our land.
Here, though the cross is lifted high
amidst the paddy fields and coconut palms
and white-clad Christians flock to the churches
when the bell calls them to worship,
our wise men have not yet seen the star
and the manger of Bethlehem
is not yet the cradle of our land.

But Christian hope never dies
and the ends of the strands of destiny
are held safe in the hands of God.
                    - Chandran Devanesan, India

Jamini Roy (1887-1972) is one of the pioneers of Indian Christian art and his influence still lingers on in India. At the age of 34 he decided to abandon the European way of living and identify more directly with his traditional Bengali roots. He began to explore new directions in his art and found inspiration in the folk art of Bengal villages. He used natural colours rather than oil and in place of canvas he used clay or lime-coated cloth on paper or wooden boards.

Part of his new style was a fish-eyed look which has been widely imitated in India. Some assumed that the wide unwinking eyes on Roy's Christ figures signified God's watchfulness with eyes never closed to the needs of men, but Roy dismissed this and pointed out that he used the same eyes on the dancing girls. To Roy, the simplicity of his style was appropriate for the humanness of Jesus. "Christ is above us," he said, "yet we can attain to him - to the higher realm of common humanity."

Jamini Roy: Flight into Egypt

The Child Jesus in the Temple

Every year the parents of Jesus went to Jerusalem for the Passover Festival. When Jesus was twelve years old, they went to the festival as usual. When the festival was over, they started back home, but the boy Jesus stayed in Jerusalem. His parents did not know this; they thought that he was with the group, so they travelled a whole day and then started looking for him among their relatives and friends. They did not find him, so they went back to Jerusalem looking for him. On the third day they found him in the Temple, sitting with the Jewish teachers, listening to them and asking questions. All who heard him were amazed at his intelligent answers. (Luke 2: 41-47)

"Once I was a guest of the Coptic Orthodox Church in Egypt. Every day, I was reminded by our Coptic friends that baby Jesus and the holy family were refugees in Egypt. Today there are about 15 million refugees around the world and the baby Jesus in Mary's arms must be fleeing from the oppressive hands of cruel rulers in many places.

Only Luke's gospel tells us about the boyhood of Jesus. 'Jesus grew both in body and in wisdom, gaining favour with God and men.' Apparently, his wisdom impressed the rabbis of the temple in Jerusalem, although he was mainly listening and asking questions of them. He did not preach to the elders as some Western artists portrayed him. He was simply participating in a religious discussion with the adults. This simple participation of youth and children is difficult in church and society today. The presence of children in church is a sign of the blessing of God and the hope of the future of the church but how many youth are permitted to participate in the activities of communities and churches today?

More than half of the 3000 million Asians are youth and children. Are we taking them seriously? Often we say, the future of Asia is in the school room, but many are deprived of the opportunity to go to school. Instead many of them are forced to work in the fields or factories. I will not mention the street children and child prostitutes but we know Jesus must be in the streets as well as in the church.

An Asian proverb says:

> If you plan for one year, sow seeds,
> If you plan for ten years, plant a tree.
> If you plan for one hundred years,
>   educate the people.

Let the young people participate in programs of the church and society. The boy Jesus is already sitting there among them."

— Toshitsugo Arai, Japan

V.S. Masoji is a Bengali Indian artist who studied at Shantiniketan, an artist's institution founded by the national poet of Bengal, Rabindranath Tagore.

V.S. Masoji: The Child Jesus in the Temple

The Baptism of Jesus

After all the people had been baptized, Jesus also was baptized. While he was praying, heaven was opened, and the Holy Spirit came down upon him in bodily form like a dove. And a voice came from heaven, "You are my own dear Son. I am pleased with you." (Luke 3: 21,22)

The Balinese have no word for art. It is a part of life itself. There is a saying that every Balinese is an artist at heart and it appears true that the arts are a part of the lifestyle of even the poorest of people on the island.

The protestant church in Bali has enthusiastically encouraged Christians to paint Christian themes, as Dr Wayan Mastra puts it, "to keep their cultural heritage, where relevant, so that they do not merely become pale imitations of their Western counterparts but grow into a strong Balinese Christian identity, mature and responsible in their faith. In this understanding the Church uses both music and dance as a means of telling the Christian story throughout Bali today."

Unlike dance and music, painting is not traditional for the whole community. Originally, art was used only in temples and palaces. Then in the 1930s, Walter Spies of Germany and Rudolf Bonnet of Holland formed artists' groups which developed the traditional arts and helped create an explosion of art that transformed parts of the island into communities dominated by artists and galleries.

"A feature of Balinese art", according to the Rev. Douglas McKenzie of Australia, "is that every corner of the canvas is filled and the paintings contain so much intricate detail, that each leaf seems carefully reproduced. Human figures reflect the grace and beauty of the island people."

The churches of Bali are full of symbolism. To enter you must cross a bridge over a small stream. This is a symbolic reminder that you pass through the waters of baptism to enter the church.

In Ketut Lasia's painting, Christ is himself baptized in a Balinese setting.

Ketut Lasia was born in 1945 in Tebesaja, a village of painters in Bali. He grew up surrounded by painters and other artists and learned the traditional skills while still a young child.

He was converted to Christianity by a Dutch missionary who taught him the love of the Bible which is now his chief source of inspiration. Lasia paints in the traditional style of Balinese artists but his themes are all found in the Bible. One of his most ambitious commissions was to paint the story of Christ in a series of 30 paintings which now cover the walls of the central Balinese church in Denpasar, Bali. The paintings are used in the Christian education program of the church.

His paintings are first drawn on canvas with a fine pen then a colouring of acrylic polymer is added.

Ketut Lasia: The Baptism of Jesus

The Temptation of Jesus

Then the Spirit led Jesus into the desert to be tempted by the Devil. After spending forty days and nights without food, Jesus was hungry. Then the Devil came to him and said, "If you are God's Son, order these stones to turn into bread."
But Jesus answered, "The scripture says, 'Man cannot live on bread alone, but needs every word that God speaks.'" (Matthew 4: 1-4)

"The choice between God and every other god is a real choice. Both make promises, both demand loyalty. It is possible to live by both. If there were no real alternative to God, all men would choose him. Indeed, God himself is the more difficult choice to justify in terms of provable results.
The chief difficulty is that God demands of us that we live by faith: faith in him, his sovereignty over the future, his sufficiency for the present; while, on the other hand, the various other gods whom we can serve appeal to us in terms of the things which we can see and the forces which we can calculate. The choice between the life of faith and the life of sight is a choice between a God whom only faith can apprehend and gods whom one has only to see to understand.
It is true that the success of the gods in fulfilling their promises is the punishment for serving them; but only they know that it is punishment who have stood face to face with the living God. It is only as we glimpse the possibilities in God that we realize the bankruptcy of what we thought was fullness when we served other gods.
Thus it is that, when we meet God, our first reaction is to run away from him in shame, to refuse him in repentance; and then cling to him in faith."

          - D.T. Niles, Sri Lanka

An Dong-Sook was born in Korea in 1922. Through the influence of another artist he was converted to Christianity and baptized in 1950. He is currently Chairman of Oriental Art at Ewha Women's University in Seoul.
His abstract art works are often based on Biblical texts. He has been experimenting with different styles and the "Temptation" (opposite) is one of his recent works. Painted in water colours in 1990 it was exhibited at the annual exhibition of Korean Christian art.

An Dong-Sook: Temptation of Christ

Calling the Disciples

As Jesus walked along the shore of Lake Galilee, he saw two fishermen, Simon and his brother Andrew, catching fish with a net. Jesus said to them, "Come with me, and I will teach you to catch men." At once they left their nets and went with him.

He went a little farther on and saw two other brothers, James and John, the sons of Zebedee. They were in their boat getting their nets ready. As soon as Jesus saw them, he called them; they left their father Zebedee in the boat with the hired men and went with Jesus. (Mark 1: 16-20)

"When the Lord calls Aboriginal men and women out of this world to do his work, He does not take away their culture or language and their true identity as Aboriginal people. He blesses them and gives them his word of commission to go into the world and preach the gospel... and he wants his disciples to communicate his words in the context of their own culture, so that the people can understand and make their response to the gospel in their own understanding. In our Aboriginal culture, when persons approach a sacred site, object, or a totem, it is as if they are approaching the tablets of stone Moses brought down from the mountain.

I believe that the role of the church is to help people develop without losing their true identity - both as individuals and, particularly in the case of the Aboriginals and Islanders, as a people."

- Djiniyini Gondarra, Australian Aboriginal

"I have been thinking a lot about the 'old way' (Aboriginal religion) and the 'new way' (Christianity). Maybe in some ways the two can go together. Maybe if the two ways do not go together we are not acting right towards God and towards ourselves."

- Deacon Boniface Perdjet, Australian Aboriginal

George Garawun is a member of the Uniting Church in Australia and lives in the Northern Territory. He is a Djining man. He painted a series of bark paintings on the life of Christ which are hanging in the church in Maningrida.

In "Calling the Disciples", he uses traditional symbols. Jesus is walking along the beach (footprints in the sand) and beckons Peter and Andrew to follow him. James and John are in the boat and Zebedee is on the beach beside a fishing net. Fish and fishing nets and water grasses on which the fish feed are also shown.

George Garawun: Calling the Disciples

God Loved the World

For God loved the world so much that he gave his only Son, so that everyone who believes in him may not die but have eternal life.   (John 3: 16,17)

"From the beginning, in many and diverse ways, Abba, Father spoke to our ancestors and prophets in Asia. But finally, Abba spoke through Jesus the son. His son through whom he also created the world. Abba so loved the world that he gave it his only son. Born in Asia of Asian flesh and blood yet filled with the spirit of Abba's totally self-giving love, Jesus committed his life to sharing this love with every person in every nation.

Today the sprawling continent of Asia is home to nearly two-thirds of the human family. Within it, the tiny percentage of Christians constitute Abba's little flock. Yet they are called to witness to his totally self-giving love symbolized by the sufferings of Jesus through his death on the cross.

The mystery of the power of Abba's love filling the human weakness of the crucified Jesus in the resurrection has irrupted into the heart of the world. The Asian sees this mystery through the unique eyes of voluntary renunciation and contemplative religiosity which coalese in a blaze of recognition of the divine mystery within human history - the divine suffuses the human.

In Abba's world, death and resurrection, human weakness and divine power, suffering and joy are not contradictory but complementary moments of life."

— Desmond De Sousa, India

Go Into Belief - Victim

Ding Fang was born in Nanjing, China in 1956. Graduating from the Nanjing Art College with a degree in oil painting, he became a teacher of art at the Nanjing Art College. Since 1988, he has been a member of the Chinese Art Academy. One of the promising young leaders of the Chinese church.

Ding Fang: Go Into Belief - Victim (Detail)

The Woman at the Well

In Samaria he came to a town named Sychar, which was not far from the field that Jacob had given to his son Joseph. Jacob's well was there, and Jesus, tired out by the journey, sat down by the well. It was about noon.

A Samaritan woman came to draw some water, and Jesus said to her, "Give me a drink of water."

The woman answered, "You are a Jew, and I am a Samaritan - so how can you ask me for a drink?" (Jews will not use the same cups and bowls that Samaritans use.)

Jesus answered, "If only you knew what God gives and who it is that is asking you for a drink, you would ask him, and he would give you life-giving water." (John 4: 5-7,9,10)

"The heart of the story is the way Jesus treated the woman of Samaria. He surprised her by asking for a drink of water. According to the cultic religious code, Jewish males were not allowed to speak to women in public; and according to the code of holiness, they were prohibited from drinking or eating from a non-Jewish vessel. It was considered 'unclean'.

But Jesus approached the woman and treated her as a person, a unique individual with certain gifts she was to share with others.

This is one way of looking at 'recovery of sight to the blind.' Jesus gave the woman sight in helping her to see what she really was. The way in which Jesus developed a friendly relationship with her, enabled her to see her own worth and to know that she had something to contribute. The blindness caused by inferiority and arrogance between the two races was wiped away.

A Thai sociologist said that 'Many people choose to live in the gloom more than in the light because the light makes one see clearly, both the things they want to see and the things they don't want to see. Many people are afraid of the light as well as the darkness. Consequently, many people decide to live in the gloom.'

When the Samaritan woman was made whole and sight was given to her, she began to see herself clearly.

> He accepted me as I am
> And delivered me from the bondage of self-hate.
> Rejoice! This is the way you worship the Lord God
> With truth and spirit! ..."

— Prakai Nontawasee, Thailand

The Ven Hatigammana Uttarananda was born in a small Sri Lankan village in 1954. Entering a Buddhist monstery against his father's wishes at the age of 10, he became a monk (Bhikku) at the age of 20. Influenced by Catholic theologian Aloysius Pieris, he became fascinated by liberation theology and studied the way Jesus dealt with people. In the account of the Samaritan woman he was aware of the breaking of many barriers. In the story, Jesus broke the barriers of ethnicity and uncleanness, both of which have great relevance in Sri Lanka today where ethnic diversities often prevent Sinhalese and Tamils using the same well. Uttarananda is also conscious of the way Jesus speaks to the woman as an equal and recognizes her human dignity. He hopes that painting this picture will help Buddhists to understand the need for the liberation of women in religion and society. The painting is oil on canvas and is owned by Rev Gudrun Lowner.

Hatigammana Uttarananda: Woman at the Well

Jesus Heals the People

Large crowds came to him, bringing with them the lame, the blind, the crippled, the dumb, and many other sick people, whom they placed at Jesus' feet; and he healed them. The people were amazed as they saw the dumb speaking, the crippled made whole, the lame walking, and the blind seeing; and they praised the God of Israel. (Matthew 15: 30,31)

"To Jesus women were human - in the fullest sense. His encounter with the bent-over woman (Luke 13: 10-17) describes in remarkable detail his recognition of her humanity. She did not ask to be healed - perhaps she had become so dehumanised by her infirmity and the attitude of people around her that she did not believe there was any hope of her standing upright. But Jesus called out to her, laid his hands on her and immediately she was made straight and glorified God. Jesus defied all norms and laws when he healed a woman on the Sabbath day. The rulers of the Synagogue were angry and criticised this breach of the law. Jesus dealt with their murmuring with surprising sharpness, 'You hypocrites' he calls them (v.15). To Jesus this woman, bound for 18 years by a debilitating physical and psychological illness, was far more important than the law. 'Daughter of Abraham' he names her (v.16), affirming all her power as an inheritor of God's liberative grace and love. To claim her place as daughter of Abraham, to be able to praise God - she has to be healed, but her demoralised psyche, her wounded heart which had lost all faith, was also healed. She thus regained her wholeness. Her salvation, to be complete, called for the healing of her body, mind and soul. An unhealthy mind can make the body very weak. We also know that it is very difficult to keep an invalid in good spirits. Jesus often emphasises the salvation dimension with the healing - 'your sins are forgiven'."

- Aruna Gnanadason and Rachel Mathew, India

Nikhil Halder was born in Bangladesh and studied art at the College of Arts and Crafts, Dacca University, Bangladesh.
He is currently working as an illustrator in the Directorate of Technical Education in Bangladesh. He is a professional artist who has exhibited widely. He painted "The Kingdom Comes" which stresses the healing ministry of Jesus for the inaugural conference of the Asian Christian Art Association

Nikhil Halder: The Kingdom Comes

The Sermon on the Mount

Jesus saw the crowds and went up a hill, where he sat down. His disciples gathered round him, and he began to teach them:
"Happy are those who know they are spiritually poor;
the Kingdom of heaven belongs to them!" (Matthew 5: 1-3)

"In the Sermon on the Mount, Christ proclaimed that God will come to root out whatever is opposed to the fullness of life - sorrow, injustice and estrangement from himself. He will come to affirm and fulfill whatever is truly human - gentleness of spirit, concern for right, purity of heart, commitment for peace, mercy to others. The Kingdom of God, therefore, is, on the one hand, liberation from all alienation, and on the other the full flowering of the human on our planet. In other words it is not only freedom *from* but also freedom *for* - freedom for creativity, community and love."
— Sebastian Kappen, India

"When I read the Sermon on the Mount, especially such passages as 'Resist not evil,' I was simply overjoyed and found my own opinion confirmed where I least expected it. The message of Jesus Christ, as I understand it, is contained in the Sermon on the Mount. The spirit of the Sermon on the Mount competes, almost on equal terms, with the Bhagavad Gita for the domination of my heart. It is that sermon which has endeared Jesus to me.
The gentle figure of Christ, so patient, so kind, so loving, so full of forgiveness that he taught his followers not to retaliate when abused or struck but to turn the other cheek - it was a beautiful example, I thought, of the perfect man."
— Mahatma Gandhi, India

Kim Hak Soo was born in Pyongyang in 1919 and studied with Kim Un Ho in Seoul in the 1940s. While recovering from a serious illness at the age of 40, he felt "a calling" to begin his life anew, returning more closely to his Christian faith.
He was encouraged by Rev Kim Yang Son to begin religious painting and he did so, using the traditional methods of old Chosun. Events are drawn in careful, correct detail using a traditional Korean brush and ink with additional colour.
To mark the centennial of the Protestant Church in Korea, Kim Hak Soo completed two large projects: 66 historical paintings of the early history of the church in Korea and an additional series on the life of Christ.
There are 36 paintings in the portrayal of the life of Christ and each shows Jesus' ministry in a Korean context. "The Sermon on the Mount" (opposite) is part of this series.

Kim Hak Soo: The Sermon on the Mount

The Sinful Woman

A Pharisee invited Jesus to have dinner with him, and Jesus went to his house and sat down to eat. In that town was a woman who lived a sinful life. She heard that Jesus was eating in the Pharisee's house, so she brought an alabaster jar full of perfume and stood behind Jesus, by his feet, crying and wetting his feet with her tears. Then she dried his feet with her hair, kissed them, and poured the perfume on them. When the Pharisee saw this, he said to himself, "If this man really were a prophet, he would know who this woman is who is touching him; he would know what kind of sinful life she lives!"
Jesus spoke up and said to him, "Simon, I have something to tell you."
"Yes, Teacher," he said, "tell me."
"There were two men who owed money to a money-lender," Jesus began. "One owed him five hundred silver coins, and the other owed him fifty. Neither of them could pay him back, so he cancelled the debts of both. Which one, then, will love him more?"
"I suppose," answered Simon, "that it would be the one who was forgiven more."...
Jesus said to the woman, "Your faith has saved you; go in peace." (Luke 7: 36-43, 50)

Jesus behaved in unorthodox ways for a Jewish man of his day. His attitude of friendship and acceptance of the despised and rejected people in society must have made a strong impression on this woman who entered the Pharisee's home to anoint Jesus' feet. Knowing how upright citizens denounced prostitutes, she nevertheless had the courage to enter, uninvited, to perform a sacrificial act of love - pouring out expensive ointment upon the feet of Jesus and drying them with her hair, oblivious or uncaring of the disapproval of the other people present.

She knelt at his feet
luxuriant black hair
    falling gently
    caressing his tired feet...
fragrant perfume
    mingling with dust and dirt
    with hair and skin...
celebrating a memorial to love.

While eyes
    with scorn
        disbelief
        disgust
see - yet don't see
A woman's faith
    celebrating
        a memorial to love.
        - Ranjini Rebera, Australia

Wu Yuen-kwei was born in China in 1947. Currently he is a senior lecturer in the Nanjing Institute of Art.

耶穌說：她
許多的罪
都赦免了
因為她的
愛多
《路加福音》
第七章四
十七節
吳元奎畫

Wu Yuen-kwei: Her Sins are Forgiven

Feeding the Multitude

When it was getting late, his disciples came to him and said, "It is already very late, and this is a lonely place. Send the people away, and let them go to the nearby farms and villages in order to buy themselves something to eat."
"You yourselves give them something to eat," Jesus answered.
They asked, "Do you want us to go and spend two hundred silver coins on bread in order to feed them?"
So Jesus asked them, "How much bread have you got? Go and see."
When they found out, they told him, "Five loaves and also two fish." (Mark 6: 35-38)

"The amazing story of Jesus feeding so many people with a very small quantity of food conceals a deep meaning: sharing must be the basis on which human community is built. It must be the heart of relationships. It is something that makes life possible.

Yet sharing was a difficult thing to practise for the people of Jesus' time. It is even more difficult for us to practise today. We know in Asia and in other parts of the world, the rich get richer and the poor get poorer. The economic system of our society and our world is not based on sharing but on power and greed. In this kind of world, God is worshipped as the god of the rich and greedy. The poor have no hope of 'raising their head above the sky' (chhut thau thi) to use a Taiwanese saying. They are regarded as losers or failures. But in actual fact the society which makes the rich, richer and poor, poorer, is a lost society. A rich world that creates starving masses is a poor world, and a religion that sides with the rich and powerful is a corrupt religion. Yet this is the kind of society and religion that has emerged in some Asian countries out of the so-called 'economic miracle.'

Sharing must be restored to the centre of a human community; it must once again become the bond of human relationships and it must be at the very heart of faith and piety. The reason is simple but profound. God, for Jesus, is the God who shares God's own self with human beings. God is love because God shares. The disclosure of God as a sharing God is good news to the poor. The assurance that God is with them and for them must be the beginning of a change in their own self-esteem and a change from passive fatalism to active participation in movements towards a more sharing and a more just society."

- Huang Po Ho, Taiwan

Zhang Wanlong, born in 1950, is a member of the Nanjing Theological Seminary art department. He was formerly a designer and factory manager with the Zhejiang Dongyang Industrial Arts Company. "Five loaves and Two Fish" is carved in wood.

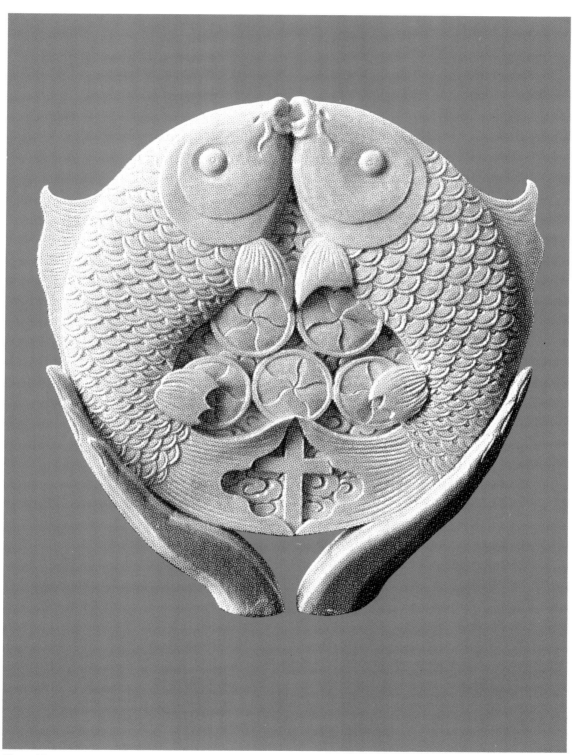

Zhang Wanlong: Five Loaves and Two Fish

The Smiling Christ

(Jesus said) "When John (the Baptist) came, he fasted and drank no wine, and everyone said, 'He has a demon in him!' When the Son of Man came, he ate and drank, and everyone said, 'Look at this man! He is a glutton and a drinker, a friend of tax collectors and other outcasts!' God's wisdom, however, is shown to be true by its results." (Matthew 11: 18,19)

There is no Biblical record of Jesus laughing, but it is impossible to believe this did not happen. His message of joy and hope had to be reflected in his complete humanity.

Japanese writer Shusaku Endo comments on this in his popular *Life of Jesus* when he speaks of Jesus attending the wedding at Cana of Galilee:

"This human-interest story of the wedding comes across with the lilt of springtime. The intention is to depict a contrast with the winter of his austerities in the forbidding wilderness of Judea. The story shows in bold relief how Jesus had survived the shortcomings of the wilderness and how he had moved beyond the ill-humored image of God upheld by the sectarians there. Jesus thoroughly enjoyed the wedding party of the young lovers. It is worthwhile to compare his laughing face putting away the drinks with the face of John the Baptist, the man clothed in animal hide fastened at the waist with a leather strap, haranguing people forever about the wrath of God. This story uncovers for us the beaming *joie de vivre* of Jesus who had moved beyond the wilderness and beyond the religious brotherhood of John.

Hunter hits the mark when he says: 'In what does the prophetic message of Jesus differ from John's? The preaching of John was a heavy burden with the old-time threat of utter destruction. But the preaching of Jesus is a song of joy.' To paraphrase a certain verse in Mark, the face of John the Baptist's disciples personified sobriety itself, whereas the disciples of Jesus were like guests at a wedding party (Mark 2: 18)."

Another Japanese writer, Shiinzo Rinzo, uses the image of mysterious laughter as a symbol of the Christian presence in the world.

Oh Hae-Chang was born in Korea in 1941. He studied at the College of Fine Arts at Seoul National University. A frequent exhibitor in group exhibitions, his work shows a Dali-like influence in an authentic Korean setting.

Oh is currently a teacher at the Taejun University, Art Department.

"The Smiling Christ" was a part of the travelling exhibition of the Asian Christian Art Association 1987/88. Painted in oils, it is now in a private collection in the United States.

Oh Hae-Chang: The Christ Smiling

The Angry Christ

It was almost time for the Passover Festival, so Jesus went to Jerusalem. There in the Temple he found men selling cattle, sheep, and pigeons, and also the money-changers sitting at their tables. So he made a whip from cords and drove all the animals out of the Temple, both the sheep and the cattle; he overturned the tables of the money-changers and scattered their coins; and he ordered the men who sold the pigeons, "Take them out of here! Stop making my Father's house a market-place!" His disciples remembered that the scripture says, "My devotion to your house, O God, burns in me like a fire." (John 2:13-17)

Because we eat roots
And flour piles up in your warehouses...
Because we live all cramped up
And your space is so abundant...
So we are not allies.

Because we are soiled
And you are shiny bright...
Because we feel suffocated
And you lock the door...
So we distrust you.

Because we are abandoned on the streets
And you own all the shade...
Because we endure floods
And you party on pleasure boats...
So we don't like you.

Because we are silenced
And you never stop nagging...
Because we are threatened
and you use violence against us...
So we say to you NO.

Because we may not choose
And you are free to make plans...
Because we have only sandals
And you are free to use rifles...
Because we must be polite
And you have jails...
So NO and NO to you.

Because we are the current of the river
And you are stones without heart...
So the water will erode away the stones.
                                        - W.S. Rendra, Indonesia

Lino Pontebon is a young artist from the Negros island of the Philippines. The area in which he lives has been the scene of considerable military action and this has added to the already hard life of the peasants.

His painting of the angry Christ captures a mood in the Philippines and reflects the prevailing anger of the people at being manipulated by forces beyond their control.

The painting became popular in many parts of the world, especially among the young. It counteracts the image of "gentle Jesus meek and mild" with the reminder that Jesus also became angry at injustice.

Lino Pontebon: The Angry Christ

The Lost Son

(The younger son left home and spent his inheritance) At last he came to his senses and said, 'All my father's hired workers have more than they can eat, and here I am about to starve! I will get up and go to my father and say, Father, I have sinned against God and against you. I am no longer fit to be called your son; treat me as one of your hired workers.' So he got up and started back to his father.

He was still a long way from home when his father saw him; his heart was filled with pity, and he ran, threw his arms round his son, and kissed him. (Luke 15: 17-20)

The story of the son who left home and spent his inheritance in reckless living has many parallels in today's society. The parable speaks to Philippine sculptor, Solomon Saprid, who has concentrated on the return home. He reflects on his work in these words:

"I have used the image of **return** in this sculpture. Obviously, it is one of the main themes of the Biblical message. Here you can think of the return of the prodigal son to his father's land. Personally, for me as an artist, this is a very important theme. We are all struggling to express what we want. We experience miserable failure and helplessness, and tend to forget our original calling as artists.

Sometimes, when we attain success and enjoy fame and honor given to an artist, we also underestimate how much God has blessed us. We constantly need to renew ourselves, to humbly accept our vocation as artist as one given by God, and we should not forget God's abundant blessings which sustain us. The work we create is limited and transitory. However, "return" is especially significant since it symbolizes that no one can be proud of what he or she has done; we must remember that it is the blessing of inspiration and hope which we will regain when we return to the original source of life."

Solomon Saprid, born March, 1917, was described by the artist Hernando Ocampo as the "Philippines' best living sculptor". It was a great tribute to one of the country's creative sculptors.

Saprid is an inspiration to those who want to begin a new life after the age of fifty. In fact he began sculpting almost by accident when he carved a piece of wood into a head of Christ. He did not begin serious sculpting until well into his 50th year but since then he has been amazingly prolific producing many works which can be seen on Manila's streets. Best-known are his "tikbalang" figures, the half-man, half-horse creature of Philippine mythology.

Saprid was one of the first enthusiastic supporters of the Asian Christian Art Association. He has been on the executive since its foundation and has produced many pieces specifically for Christian art exhibitions.

"The Return" was made in direct metal sculpture by melting and welding strips of brass to form a design. The heat comes from the use of oxygen and acetylene. It was presented to the Asian Christian Art Association at its most recent executive meeting in Chiengmai, 1990.

Solomon Saprid: The Return

The Good Samaritan

Jesus said, "There was once a man who was going down from Jerusalem to Jericho when robbers attacked him, stripped him, and beat him up, leaving him half dead. It so happened that a priest was going down that road; but when he he saw the man, he walked on by, on the other side. In the same way a Levite also came along, went over and looked at the man, and then walked on by, on the other side. But a Samaritan who was travelling that way came upon the man, and when he saw him, his heart was filled with pity..." (Luke 10: 30-33)

"The parable as it is told to us sees only the victim - the robber is outside the frame. And looking at the victim it is easy to love. You can love in simple and individual relief or, as one apocryphal commentary says, the good Samaritan kept coming week after week, and there was victim after victim, and he says, 'This is a social problem! I'd better get around to my fellow good Samaritans, set up a trust fund and put up a Good Samaritan Hospital, because an institutional and social approach is necessary for massive and quantitative social problems.' That is still no problem so long as it is just the victim.

Go to the next frame: The good Samaritan runs after the robber and says, 'Don't do that again, will you?' You can counsel the robber and even understand the humanity of the robber. The robber could very well say, 'Yes that is a problem, but I also have problems, My children are into drugs.'

Apocryphal commentary number two says: The good Samaritan came too early. The robber was still there robbing the victim, and the victim was not quite a victim yet - the victim was resisting. The good Samaritan saw both sides, not only one and said, 'I must love, but how?' What he saw was the process of oppression, not just the crime. He saw two sides in conflict and he wanted to love.

How to resolve it? The first step is to take sides in the struggle. Not by rushing into the fray but by exercising a calculated judgement that the situation is complex, I might not have all the data, but there is something very obvious - one side is getting the worst of it.

- Edicio de la Torre, Philippines

Kim Ki-Chang was born in Seoul, Korea, February 1914. After studying art, he married Pak Nae-hyon who is herself an artist. Together they held many joint exhibitions in USA and Korea.

In 1972 he became Professor of Painting at Sudo Women's Teachers College in Seoul.

Kim travels widely and has held exhibitions in several parts of the world. He paints in a traditional Korean style and produced a number of art works to illustrate the Korean version of the New Testament in 1970.

The "Good Samaritan" (opposite) is painted with water colours on silk.

Kim Ki-Chang: The Good Samaritan

The Lost Coin

(Jesus told them this parable) "Suppose a woman who has ten silver coins loses one of them - what does she do? She lights a lamp, sweeps her house, and looks carefully everywhere until she finds it. When she finds it, she calls her friends and neighbours together and says to them, 'I am so happy I found the coin I lost. Let us celebrate!' In the same way, I tell you, the angels of God rejoice over one sinner who repents." (Luke 15:8-10)

"The parable of the lost coin is a short and unique story. It is found between two other parables, the 'lost sheep' and the 'lost son'. In these two parables the actors are men who are shown to care for those who are lost. If one sheep is lost the good shepherd cares for the one who is lost. When the younger son is lost, the father cares for the lost son. The Bible frequently uses images of the shepherd or the father for God. It was a new thing in faith history when God was shown to come out and search for those who are lost. The story of the lost coin is even more revolutionary. Jesus is telling us that God is persistently seeking sinners. Can God be seen as a woman? Why not? In the parable Jesus uses the image of a woman who searches for a small coin until she finds it. Her persistence is remarkable because a small coin does not have a great value. But the woman still invests all her time and energy in the search.

It is good news to millions of suffering, insignificant and marginalized people in the world to know that God cares for them. The majority of Christians in the Indian sub-continent come from the untouchable class. This story gives them tremendous encouragement.

To all the world's marginalized people the parable of the lost coin is attractive good news."

- John V. Samuel, Pakistan

"The whole creation is beloved of God.
Like the woman who swept and cleaned her house in search of a lost coin we affirm that God cares for even the last little detail of this, God's household, into which we are placed. Women who care for life and nurture it in the daily events of their lives have always been a part of that loving relationship towards all that is and the whole of creation."

- Women's Statement to the Conference on Justice Peace and Integrity of Creation.

Saw Edward was born in Burma (Myanmar) in 1945 and studied art at the Myanmar State School of Fine Art.

He is now working for the Episcopal Church (Church of England) in the Province of Myanmar as Communications Director.

He has done illustrations for church publications and some oil painting of Biblical themes.

He uses the traditional Burmese style of art in order to communicate more directly with the local people. This is based on rhythm of lines, the same tone in colours, no light or shade and very little perspective.

"The Lost Coin" is painted in oil on canvas.

Saw Edward: The Lost Coin

The Ten Girls

"Once there were ten girls who took their oil lamps and went out to meet the bridegroom. Five of them were foolish, and the other five were wise. The foolish ones took their lamps but did not take any extra oil with them...

It was already midnight when the cry rang out, 'Here is the bridegroom! Come and meet him!' The ten girls woke up and trimmed their lamps. Then the foolish ones said to the wise ones, 'Let us have some of your oil, because our lamps are going out.' 'No, indeed,' the wise ones answered, 'there is not enough for you and for us. Go to the shop and buy some for yourself.' "...

And Jesus concluded, "Be on your guard then, because you do not know the day or the hour."
(Matthew 25: 1b-3,6-9,13)

A wedding is the cause of great excitement. There is always much to do - guest lists to compile and catering to organize. Being a bridesmaid is a special honour.

According to Palestinian marriage custom the bridesmaids stand along the road, their lamps lighting the way for the bridegroom.

In the parable, the bridegroom was delayed and the bridesmaids fell asleep. When it was finally announced that the bridegroom was coming the bridesmaids who had brought enough oil for their lamps began the procession to meet him with their lamps burning brightly. The foolish bridesmaids who had been very casual about their responsibilities ran out of oil and had to try and buy some. The bridegroom welcomed the prepared and turned the foolish away. All of us are invited to share in the nuptial celebrations of heaven.We prepare ourselves through following God's law, serving those in need, working for the poor and developing our own spiritual life.

But like the foolish bridesmaids, many fail to use these means of preparation. We doze and sleep contentedly, holding empty oil lamps in our hands. When the bridegroom comes we are unprepared. At that moment, each of us stands on our own merits - there can be no borrowing the oil of merit from others. Now is the time for us to knock on the door and call on God for his mercy and kindness. God's love will open the eyes of our understanding, making us aware of the many possibilities of encountering Christ in our daily lives. When our lamps are topped with faith and love, they light the way for Christ whom we meet in prayer and sacrament, in people and in the daily experiences of life.

- Gael O'Leary, Aotearoa/New Zealand

Yoshie Kawakami was born in Osaka, Japan in 1903. She studied pharmacology and then shifted her interest to art.

She has membership in Shundei-Kai, a Japanese Painters' Association and exhibits widely.

Kawakami experienced conversion in 1956 and received baptism at the age of 53. She is a member of the Himematsu United Church of Christ in Japan.

Yoshie Kawakami: Ten Virgins

Workers in the Harvest

As Jesus saw the crowds, his heart was filled with pity for them, because they were worried and helpless, like sheep without a shepherd. So he said to his disciples, "The harvest is large, but there are few workers to gather it in. Pray to the owner of the harvest that he will send out workers to gather in his harvest." (Matthew 9: 36-38)

"At this time Lord, we are especially thankful for the golden ripe grain and for the hundred kinds of red fruits. Where do they come from? The farmers who take them into their barns think they are the result of their own labours. But, O Lord, they are yours. To sustain our lives you have given us the sunshine and the proper rain; by these we sustain our lives and for them we are grateful. Just as the farmers, following natural laws, are busy at the time of sowing so that they will reap, so may we follow the laws which you have established and sow righteousness every day. Amen."

- Korean farmer's prayer

"Lord help us realise that our Christianity is like a rice field: when it is newly-planted, the paddies are prominent; but as the plants take root and grow taller, these dividing paddies gradually vanish and soon there appears one vast continuous field. So give us roots of love and make us grow in Christian fellowship and service, so that your will be done in our lives. Through Jesus your Son, Amen."

- Philippine farmer's prayer

"A thousand autumns have passed,
　　the waters stay the same.
A thousand generations have looked at the moon
　　and she is still herself.
We know all these things
　　only the human heart
　　remains a mystery."

- Nguyen Trai, Vietnam

George Keyt was born in Kandy, Sri Lanka in 1901 and studied at Trinity College. Influenced by the poetry of Bengali poet Rabindranath Tagore and the painting of post-impressionists like Braque and Picasso, he still retains his Sri Lanka tradition in the use of colour and in the outlines of figures. His powerful painting of "Christ the King" appeared in Christian Art in Asia.

George Keyt: The Sower

The Servant

Jesus called them all together and said, "You know that the rulers of the heathen have power over them, and the leaders have complete authority. This, however, is not the way it shall be among you. If one of you wants to be great, he must be the servant of the rest; and if one of you wants to be first, he must be your slave - like the Son of Man, who did not come to be served, but to serve and to give his life to redeem many people." (Matthew 20: 25-28)

"In our painting and sculpture, our hymns and prayers the image of Jesus as the servant Lord needs to be given greater prominence. We need to make our places of worship much more places where service is rendered to others; and make places where service is rendered to others in everyday life also places of worship. Our rites and ceremonies, our forms of worship must, through shared silence and shared actions and gestures, convey the mystery and majesty of the lowliness of the servant Lord, rather than the pomp and panoply of a reigning monarch."
- Lakshman Wickremesinghe, Sri Lanka

"The servant is called upon to respond bodily to the intense physical suffering of the people. He has to release and restore the prisoners, the broken and the maimed, secure in the conviction that the new age belongs to them.
The role of the servant is difficult in another sense. He knows that in the present, the rulers are using his own suffering and self-sacrifice for their own purposes. He belongs to those on the periphery who are sacrificed for those in the centre. All that sustains him now is the conviction that he will be vindicated and that self-sacrifice, the quality of giving oneself as a ransom for many, rather than the violence which sacrifices others, will characterize the new age."
- D. Preman Niles, Sri Lanka

Chao Chien-ming is a full-time artist in China. He works with the Nantong Academy of Chinese Traditional Painting in Jiangsu Province.

耶穌說
你們中間誰
願為大就必
作你們的用人
正如人子來
不是要受人
的服事乃是
要服事人並且
要捨命作
多人的贖價
馬太福音第廿章
廿六、廿八節 壬戌年畫

Chao Chien-ming: Not to be Served But to Serve

121

The Lord's Prayer (i)

(Jesus said) "When you pray, do not use a lot of meaningless words, as the pagans do, who think that God will hear them because their prayers are long. Do not be like them. Your Father already knows what you need before you ask him. This, then, is how you should pray:
'Our Father in heaven:
May your holy name be honoured;...
(Matthew 6: 7-9)

"When we pray 'Hallowed be thy name' in all the world, we mean that it should be recognized as such everywhere. For we must know that it is not in our power to add or detract from God's holiness. God is what he is; as he spoke to Moses, 'I am who I am'. (Exodus 3: 14). What is meant by the petition is: Let God's name be hallowed in us and by us. This is done in two ways: by words of praise and by acts pleasing to God.

Praise of God in prayer and song is the most natural way of expressing and acknowledging God's holiness.

There is a long history of reverent religious music in praise of God in the Indian *bhakti* tradition from the Tamil poets of the seventh century A.D. The Christian churches have adopted the style of these lyrics to express loving devotion to God. An example is the popular Hindi lyric: Jaye jaye Yishu:

> Victory to Jesus, victory to Jesus:
> Hail to the conqueror of death.
> Hail to the victor supreme,
> The creator, the maintainer, the saviour.

God's name is hallowed by acts that are pleasing to him. This was the burden of the message of the prophets of Israel.

God's name is hallowed where justice is upheld. Justice is usually carried on in terms of law, but Christian justice is a guardian over law itself. It is opposed not only to lawlessness but also to bad and discriminatory law. Christ is the conscience of all law. Ideal justice is opposed to all kinds of favouritism and discrimination."
                                             - Herbert Jai Singh, India

Paul Navaratne lives in the central mountains of Sri Lanka where he was born in 1909.

After study in Mysore at the Sri Chamaragendra Institute he returned to Sri Lanka and joined other artists in support of Bishop Lakasa de Mel's plan to indigenize the church.

Since 1949 Navaratne has been in Gunnapana, directing the Kandyan Handicrafts and Woodwork Institute.

The simple style of his watercolour paintings draws on the ordinary symbols of daily life in Sri Lanka. The Sinhala (Kandyan) influence on his work is a deliberate choice to enable him to communicate with local people.

His painting "Hallowed be Thy Name" combines light from three sources flowing in a confluence of praise. The candles are surrounded by precious stones, part of Sri Lanka's natural resources and a stylised lotus in the frame adds to the act of adoration.

Paul Navaratne: Hallowed be Thy Name

The Lord's Prayer (ii)

...may your kingdom come;
may your will be done on earth
as it is in heaven...
(Matthew 6:10)

"Jesus was fully aware of the aspirations of the common people. He was one of them. To them he preached the Kingdom of God. Through them he sought to communicate the gospel of salvation to others beyond their fold. Although he was not a fanatic political revolutionary, he was fully aware of the contradictions between the existing political reality under Roman domination and the popular hope for the coming of a political Messiah. He was also conscious of his mission to awaken people to the fact that with his coming, God's Kingdom had broken into human history.

The historical context in which Jesus preached the message of the Kingdom of God was not that of the sophisticated elites of Jewish society. Rather it was that of the common people. Both the custodians of institutional piety and those who controlled the levers of political and economic power shunned him. On many occasions he was an offence to them. But his gospel of the Kingdom of God was indeed good news to the sick, disabled, alienated and oppressed. The multitude of ordinary people (the *ochlos/minjung*) flocked around him (Mark 2:4). It is not very clear why they followed him. They may have been attracted to him because of his charismatic qualities; others may have seen in him an opportunity to realize their personal aspirations. Or they may have found a true friend in him who accepted and cared about society's outcasts: publicans, prostitutes and sinners. When the ruling elites criticized and attacked Jesus the people (*ochlos*) rallied round him (Mark 2: 4-6, 3: 2-21, 11: 18-27) It was only through bribery that the rulers were able to incite them at the trial of Jesus. The rulers were, in fact, afraid of the people."

- Park Sang Jung, Korea

Viboon Leesuwan is an artist and teacher. Born in Angthong Province, Thailand, he graduated from the University of Fine Art in Bangkok.

He has been a guiding force among Thai artists in the development of abstract art using colour and texture.

He has sought to open his students' eyes to understand traditional folk art and Thai handicraft in a new way. He has given special attention to colour and when he was invited to portray the coming of God's kingdom for a conference, he felt it could only be depicted in an abstract form letting the colours speak for themselves.

The work is a silk screen print in the collection of the Asian Christian Art Association.

Viboon Leesuwan: Your Kingdom Come

The Lord's Prayer (iii)

...Give us today the food we need.
Forgive us the wrongs we have done,
as we forgive the wrongs that others have done to us.
Do not bring us to hard testing,
but keep us safe from the Evil One.
(Matthew 6: 11-13)

"At the table of life we share most disproportionately indeed. Some go hungry. Others are besottedly full. The quality of rice we eat is according to the wealth or penury we bring with us to the table. And we eat only with people of our own kind. We do not, as Paul sorrowfully writes, have enough respect for the community of God. We embarrass the poor outrageously. This is our world. A world of plenty and want; of staggering riches and even more staggering poverty. And into this confused and confusing world comes the stranger seeking to pitch his tent among us."
- Bishop Francisco Claver, Philippines

Heaven is rice
As we cannot go to heaven alone
We should share with one another
As we all share the light of the heavenly stars
We should share and eat rice together
Heaven is rice
When we eat and swallow rice
Heaven dwells in our body
Rice is heaven
Yes, rice is something
We should eat together.
- Kim Chi Ha, Korea

Penniless. . .
A while
Without food
I can live;
But it breaks my heart
To know
I cannot give.

Penniless. . .
I can share my rags,
But I -
I cannot bear to hear
Starved children cry.
- Toyohiko Kagawa, Japan

Vincente Manansala was born 1910 in Pampanga, Philippines. After graduating from the University of the Philippines he became one of the pioneers of modern art in his country. He was part of a group known as the Thirteen Moderns and the Neo-realists. He developed a transparent cubist style apparent in the work opposite.
Manansala was constantly returning to Christian themes in his art and his work is seen in many churches.
He died in August 1981.

Vincente Manansala: Our Daily Bread

Palm Sunday

The large crowd that had come to the Passover Festival heard that Jesus was coming to Jerusalem. So they took branches of palm trees and went out to meet him, shouting, "Praise God! God bless him who comes in the name of the Lord! God bless the King of Israel!" Jesus found a donkey and rode on it, just as the scripture says. (John 12: 12-14)

"Jesus chose to enter Jerusalem riding on a donkey - a colt. There is no doubt it was a deliberate symbol. Was it to poke fun at the pretentions of the powerful? Would they be expecting the Messiah to ride a white horse into the city?

But it is the donkey that speaks most powerfully of the ministry of Jesus. He always seemed to choose the weak and the lowly as the symbols of his calling. The lamb and the sheep, the dove and the donkey are all weak and powerless creatures.

By his action, Jesus was saying something about power and powerlessness. The humility of his action stands in contrast to the crowd's expectation of him as a conqueror. In the entry to Jerusalem, God is identified with the poor rather than the rich, with the humble against the proud, with those who love against those who hate, with peace against war. All the virtues which we tend to see as weak are the ones which he claims to be strong. He gives up power and in his powerlessness shows the greater strength.

In many Bible commentaries, this event is decribed as "the triumphal entry". This statement is a complete misnomer. It arose in medieval times when the church was obsessed with temporal power.

The truth is lost if we associate this event with triumphalism. Jesus entered Jerusalem with all the symbols of simple humility. His actions were a mockery of the things the world associates with power.

But it is in his humility that real strength resides. In his weakness is our strength."

- Ron O'Grady, Aotearoa/New Zealand

Gako Ota is the professional name of artist, Sute Ota, a pioneer in the use of flower arrangements in Japanese churches. Brought up in a rural mountain village in Hyogo she would climb the mountains behind her home to collect wild flowers. Later she moved to Kyoto city and worked in an advertising agency but her first love was always ikebana - flower arrangement.
After World War II she arranged the flowers at the altar of her local church every Sunday.
Her portrayal of Palm Sunday makes use of concrete blocks which provide a strong contrast to the palm fronds.
She died in 1972.

Gako Ota: Palm Sunday

Washing the Feet

Jesus knew that the Father had given him complete power; he knew that he had come from God and was going to God. So he rose from the table, took off his outer garment, and tied a towel round his waist. Then he poured some water into a basin and began to wash the disciples' feet and dry them with the towel round his waist. He came to Simon Peter, who said to him, "Are you going to wash my feet, Lord?"
Jesus answered him, "You do not understand now what I am doing, but you will understand later." (John 13: 3-7)

In the Workers' Mass of the Christian Workers' Fellowship of Sri Lanka, the celebration concludes with a chant which links the Lord's Supper with the calling to serve the people:

> We have made memorial of your death,
>   O Christ
> Your resurrection's symbol we have seen
> Now filled with your undying life
> In this sacrament we have been
> United to you and one another.
> As we in fellowship have shared this food -
> Your gift and symbols too of the people's work
> So may all for the common good
> Share in the products of our earth!
> With this manna for our march we go
> Hopefully, joyfully to serve you more
> In the struggle to free all people
> And in that struggle power to wrest
> For the working people
> In the interests of all.
> In this way by your grace we can
> Help build a new society, new man,
> A new heaven and a new earth
> In your strength, we now go forth.

From the Liturgy of Malabar (Syriac):

> Strengthen for service, Lord, the hands
> That holy things have taken;
> Let ears that now have heard thy songs
> To clamour never waken.

Jyoti Sahi of Bangalore, India, has probably been one of the most influential Christian artists in Asia in recent years.
Not only is he an innovative and creative artist at home in many different forms of art, but he also has a sharp theological insight into art and culture and has expressed this in numerous articles and lectures. Jyoti has wrestled for years on the meaning of dialogue between Christianity and indigenous Indian religions.This has been well expressed in his art and we have been permitted to see something of the personal side of this struggle through his writings in Image and in recent books, "The Serpent and the Child" and "Stepping Stones". Several small booklets of his reflections and art have been published in Europe.
Jyoti lives in an ashram near Bangalore in India where his wife Jane has a small village school. Several Indian artists have come periodically to live and paint in the ashram.
Many of Jyoti's works are found in churches and galleries and some deal with complex religious themes. We have chosen a simple example of his work for this book: Jesus washing the feet of the disciple in the parameters of the leaf of the sacred bodhi tree.

Jyoti Sahi: Washing the Feet

The Betrayal of Christ

Jesus was still speaking when Judas, one of the twelve disciples, arrived. With him was a large crowd armed with swords and clubs and sent by the chief priests and the elders... Judas went straight to Jesus and said, "Peace be with you, Teacher," and kissed him. Jesus answered, "Be quick about it, friend!" (Matthew 26: 47,49,50)

Judas, the disciple of Christ
Judas, the betrayer of Christ

Judas who repented for his sin
Judas who paid for his sin with his own life.

Can we ever understand or know
The violence and passion of this man -
The violence of his intention
And the passion of his love?

Perhaps, more than any other
He recognized Jesus as the Messiah;
If he did
How could he believe
The Messiah could die?

Can we ever understand or know
Why Judas was Judas?
                            - Nalini Jayasuriya, Sri Lanka

The worries of Judas are a common human position before the challenging situation brought about by Jesus. Judas ultimately put in his lot with the religious and social establishment of the day. In a time of crisis he opted for the traditional religion and for the Roman imperialists for whom the life and message of Jesus was a threat. Judas fell victim to power, corruption, intrigue and conspiracy.

In the end, he was neither with Jesus nor satisfied with the authorities. His betrayal of Jesus was one of indecision, greed for money, subservience to power and sneakish conspiracy. When we see the inner conflict in his being, we can understand the price the other apostles had to pay in being loyal to the new religion.   - Tissa Balasuriya, Sri Lanka

Nalini Jayasuriya grew up in Sri Lanka and later studied art in England. She experimented with many forms of art but is best known for her acrylic and pastel paintings on Biblical themes.
In 1979 she received a scholarship to do a year's research and writing at Yale Divinity School, USA. At the end of that time she became the Elizabeth Luce visiting Professor appointed by the Board of Christian Higher Education in Asia.
She has written extensively on art subjects and held many exhibitions. In 1989 she took up her current position as Associate for Worship and the Arts of the Presbyterian Church, USA in Louisville, Kentucky.
Her popular paintings are mostly produced in oil pastel.
In her painting of Judas (opposite) the tortured face of the disciple reflects some of the complexities of the man who betrayed Jesus.

Nalini Jayasuriya: Judas

Meetings

"My commandment is this: love one another, just as I love you. The greatest love a person can have for his friends is to give his life for them. And you are my friends if you do what I command you. I do not call you servants any longer, because a servant does not know what his master is doing. Instead, I call you friends, because I have told you everything I have heard from my Father... This, then, is what I command you: love one another."
(John15: 12-15,17)

The last days of Jesus' life were filled with incidents. He met and spoke to a great number of people in differing circumstances.

The painting opposite illustrates five of these encounters. In the garden of Gethsemane, Judas, a friend and disciple led the soldiers to Jesus and betrayed him with a kiss; on the road to calvary Jesus met his mother; also on the road he encountered other women of Jerusalem who empathised with him in his suffering; at the cross, one of the men crucified, a thief, asked Jesus to remember him when he came into his Kingdom and finally there was the last meeting when friends took his body and laid it in the tomb.

Gael O'Leary takes these five random encounters to remind us of the circumstances in which we meet Jesus today. In our own lives and in the lives of friends, times of betrayal, suffering and pain, life and death, can all be moments when we meet Jesus. Such encounters reflect our own struggles with the faith. There are times when we betray our own high ideals and turn our backs on a commitment we have made. In other situations the suffering of humanity seems so great that we feel powerless to act and we can only respond like Mary and the women by standing in solidarity and loving support. Sometimes we are invited to minister to criminals and try to offer life and hope to those who carry crosses of their own making. And at the end, like the disciples, we have to find in the pain and separation of death a rich source of new life. Our sadness and grief give way to peace and hope.

Gael O'Leary is a member of the Sisters of Mercy in Auckland, New Zealand. Born in Te Awamutu in 1948, she trained as a teacher specialising in art.

Her bronze wall sculptures have been commissioned by churches and hospitals. She has also developed her skills in painting and print-making and uses the print technique for making social comment on issues of the day. Her prints on unemployment, the need for housing and hungry children are widely used to support organisations who work for the poor in New Zealand. She writes that she "seeks to express Gospel values in a way that speaks for today and makes social comment."

In "Meetings" (opposite), she uses oils to dramatic effect.

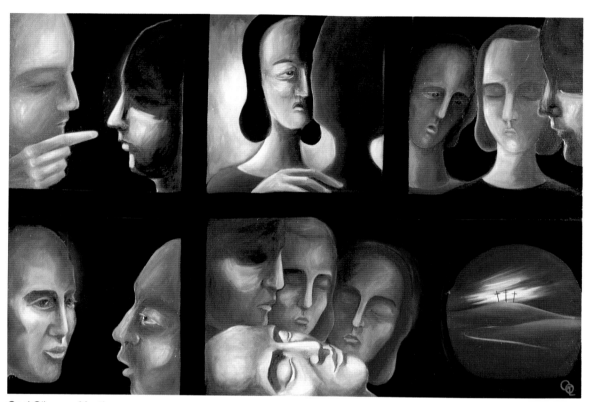

Gael O'Leary: Meetings

The Crown of Thorns

The soldiers took Jesus inside to the courtyard of the governor's palace and called together the rest of the company. They put a purple robe on Jesus, made a crown out of thorny branches, and put it on his head. Then they began to salute him: "Long live the King of the Jews!" They beat him over the head with a stick, spat on him, fell on their knees, and bowed down to him. When they had finished mocking him, they took off the purple robe and put his own clothes back on him. Then they led him out to crucify him. (Mark 15: 16-20)

What happens when an innocent person is forced into captivity, bound, blindfolded, humiliated and threatened with mental and physical harm and possibly death? This was the question which plagued Singapore sculptor Ng Eng Teng when he heard of the story of 51 American hostages held in Iran from November 4, 1979.

As he tried to depict the experience of their suffering, Ng showed the victim standing tall for his people and not losing his integrity. The victim wears a crown of thorns which symbolises sacrifice of self for others. Barbed wire, the sign of division and separation, is used to make the crown for the victim.

In the suffering of innocent victims, we see the suffering of Christ - the innocent man who died for all people.

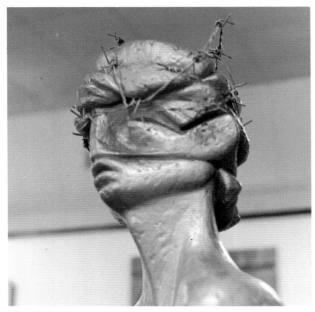

The Victim

Ng Eng Teng is a graduate of the Nanyang Academy of Fine Arts in Singapore. After study in England and Ireland he returned to Singapore and experimented with several forms of art including pottery, oil-painting and Chinese brush painting. His main concentration, however, has been sculpture using a cement fondu technique which enables him to make dramatic rounded sculptures of human forms. His work is found in many public places in Singapore including the departure hall of Changi International airport.

He says: "My works are reflections of my thoughts and experiences in visual form. The creative impulses come not from the environment immediately around, but from a universal world and from my own inner tensions. My sculptures speak of individual alienation, pain, poverty, loss of life as well as justice and love."

At the first exhibition of the Singapore Christian Artists Association his sculpture "The Victim" created much interest in the community. Although it speaks of prisoners everywhere, the crown of thorns point to the suffering of Jesus.

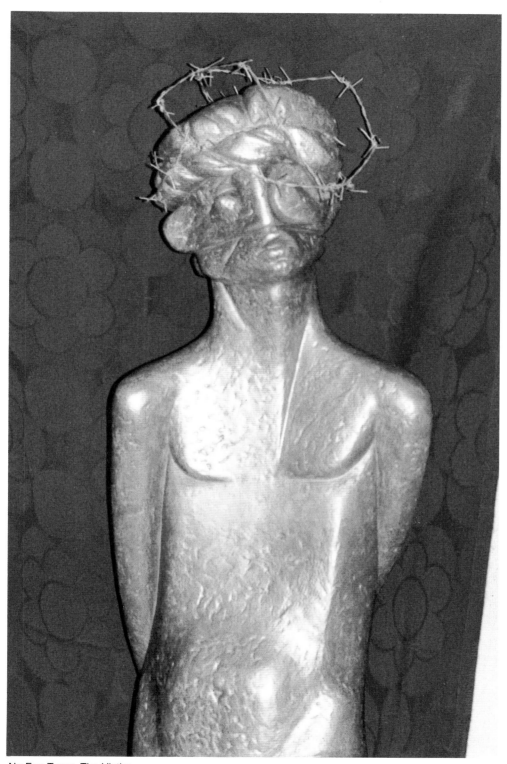

Ng Eng Teng: The Victim

The Road to Calvary

The soldiers led Jesus away, and as they were going, they met a man from Cyrene named Simon who was coming into the city from the country. They seized him, put the cross on him, and made him carry it behind Jesus. (Luke 23: 26)

Miriam-Rose Ungunmerr explains the symbolism of the Stations of the Cross: "The third stop shows Jesus falling for the first time (below). In Jesus' weakened state the weight of the cross forces him to fall. The patterns on his body show the physical stress he is under. The circles on his head indicate the pain and sorrow locked up inside him. The patterns on the cross show the increasing weight on his shoulders. In the Fifth Station, Simon of Cyrene helps Jesus carry the cross (opposite). When Simon takes hold of the cross, his body merges with that of Jesus. The pattern on Jesus' head is open: he is giving grace to Simon to strengthen him. When Simon took hold of the cross, something happened inside him: the sun rose inside his head, his mind burst with a new belief, he became a new man. The resurrection had already begun." Miriam-Rose prays: "Jesus you take your heavy cross. It gives you pain. Help all who suffer. Forgive us for the pain we give you and others."

Jesus Falls the First Time (**Detail**)

Miriam-Rose Ungunmerr was a member of the Daly River Mission church in Australia's Northern Territory. When it was being re-decorated in 1974 she was invited to paint a series of Stations of the Cross. It is unusual for an Aboriginal woman to paint since this is usually the task of the men, but she accepted the challenge and produced a remarkable series of paintings which, like other Aboriginal art, uses symbols to go beyond external shapes to inner meanings and emotions. The Stations of the Cross were painted in acrylic paint on burnie board.

Miriam-Rose was born in 1950 and after mission schooling trained as a teacher. She worked with the Northern Territory Education Department for some time as an adviser in Aboriginal art and craft. She has written and illustrated a number of books.

She is a foundation member of the Asian Christian Art Association and attended the first conference in Bali.

In 1984, Dove Communications, Melbourne, published "Australian Stations of the Cross" the full collection of the Daly River paintings.

Miriam-Rose Ungunmerr: Simon of Cyrene Helps Jesus Carry the Cross

Women of Jerusalem

A large crowd of people followed him; among them were some women who were weeping and wailing for him. Jesus turned to them and said, "Women of Jerusalem! Don't cry for me, but for yourselves and your children. For the days are coming when people will say, 'how lucky are the women who never had children, who never bore babies, who never nursed them!' That will be the time when people will say to the mountains, 'Fall on us!' and to the hills, 'Hide us!' For if such things as these are done when the wood is green, what will happen when it is dry?" (Luke 23: 27-31)

The agony of separation is the moment for anguish and weeping. In the suffering of Asia the road to calvary is often traversed. Here is an eye witness account of the time in the 1960s when Tamil workers were repatriated from Sri Lanka:

"There was much weeping and wailing. Some of the women were beating their breasts, knowing that they would never see their homeland again, the place where they were born, the country-side where they had toiled, the home where they were married, where they had given birth to their children, ate, drank, danced and slept, performed their religious ceremonies and buried their dead. Destined to see these familiar places no more they were as if they were being torn apart, severed in two."

While waiting to be deported, one of the women wrote her thoughts in Tamil:

> The rulers alone decided
> That we leave this land
> And go across the sea
> And the loved one is separated
> From the beloved...
>
> I do not know, O God
> What is there in store for me
> Only let me have your grace
> To live with your blessing.
>   - V. Mookan

J. Elizalde Navarro was born in the Philippines May, 1924. He taught at the College of Architecture and Fine Arts in the University of Santo Tomas, Manila. In 1969 he also taught for a year in Sydney, Australia. Better known as a sculptor than painter, he has represented the Philippines at two biennials in Sao Paulo, Brazil in the category of sculpture.
Navarro's "Weeping Women of Jerusalem" painted in oil and acrylic on canvas was painted, he said, "to symbolize the sadness and the grieving of humankind all over the world for injustices, inequities and evil foisted on them by others."
It is now in the collection of the Asian Christian Art Association.

J. Elizalde Navarro: Weeping Women of Jerusalem

Jesus is Crucified

They took Jesus to a place called Golgotha, which means "The Place of the Skull." There they tried to give him wine mixed with a drug called myrrh, but Jesus would not drink it. Then they crucified him and divided his clothes among themselves, throwing dice to see who would get which piece of clothing. It was nine o'clock in the morning when they crucified him. (Mark 15: 22-25)

Following a rally on Human Rights Day, December 10, 1979, eight human rights proponents in Taiwan were arrested and imprisoned. Ten others including the general secretary of the Presbyterian Church, Dr C.M. Kao, a Lutheran pastor, Wu Wen and the principal of the Calvin Theological Institute for Women, Miss Lin Wen-cheng gave sanctuary to one of the accused and were also imprisoned. During the trial and their imprisonment most of the prisoners wrote poems and letters of encouragement to their friends. Lin Hung Hsuan, a graduate of Tainan Theological College wrote:

"As we remember Jesus' crucifixion today, we must, at the same time, ask God's love and mercy for our people in their time of trouble. We also pray for people in the world who are oppressed and whose life is bitter. May the sins that create pain and torment for people disappear soon. May God's justice and mercy fill human community. May more people be able to envision the brighter side of the world. And may more people testify to this wonderful good news.

In this way, people will be able to find meaning in their lives, and those men and women who gave their lives for the peace and well-being of humanity will be always remembered for their noble deeds. In this way too, the cross, as an instrument for punishing convicts, will become a symbol of the highest honour."

> The fire does not depart
> yet still new shoots outsurge.
> The kindling flames will start
> and blossoms fair emerge.
> -C.M. Kao

Lutheran pastor, Wu Wen, speaking at his trial, said:
> "If mercy becomes sedition,
> our society has no love."

Yu Yu Yang is considered Taiwan's leading sculptor. After study in Japan, China and Italy he returned to Taiwan to develop a unique form of art which he called "lifescapes". Drawing on the traditional Chinese yearning for the unity of people with nature he created an environment which is a functional adornment to modern surroundings. His lifescapes have been used at international Expos and in temples and hotels throughout Asia as well as Europe and the United States.

A recipient of numerous awards for his design work, he has, in recent years, adopted new technologies with enthusiasm and was one of the first to expolore the world of abstract laser art.

He attended the Asian Christian Art Association Conference in the Philippines in March 1984. Crucifixion (opposite) is a graphic combination of painting and sculpture.

Yu Yu Yang: Crucifixion

Beneath the Cross

When they came to the place called "The Skull," they crucified Jesus there, and the two criminals, one on his right and the other on his left. Jesus said, "Forgive them, Father! They don't know what they are doing." (Luke 23: 33,34)

Here is the footstool and there rest thy feet
Where live the poorest and lowliest and lost

When I try to bow to thee my obeisance
cannot reach down to the depths
　　where thy feet rest.
Among the poorest and lowliest and lost.
　　　　　　　- Rabindranath Tagore, Bengal

"O God, the Parent of our Lord Jesus Christ, and our Parent: thou who art to us both Father and Mother: We who are thy children draw around thy lotus feet to worship thee. Thy compassion is as the fragrance of the lotus. Though thou art enthroned in the heavens, we may draw nigh to thee; for thy feet stand upon the earth where we humans dwell. Thy son, our Lord, was man.

We see thy compassion in Jesus. He gives content to the Hindu name for thee - Siva, the kindly one. He gives significance to the Moslem address of thee - Allah, the Merciful. He embodies in the Godhead what the Buddhist worship in the Buddha - compassion itself.

Thou God of all the world, let our history teach us that we belong to Thee alone and that thou alone dost belong to us. And thou art enough, for in thee we sinners find sonship and daughterhood again - the one thing we most need. "　　　- D.T. Niles, Sri Lanka

Anthony Doss is on the staff of the College of Arts and Crafts, Madras. His paintings combine Biblical themes with the spontaneous vitality of indigenous Indian art.

Anthony Doss: Adoration

He Calls for Elijah

At three o'clock Jesus cried out with a loud shout, *"eloi, eloi, lema sabachthani?"* which means, "My God, my God, why did you abandon me?"
Some of the people there heard him and said, "Listen, he is calling for Elijah!" One of them ran up with a sponge, soaked it in cheap wine, and put it on the end of a stick. Then he held it up to Jesus' lips and said, "Wait! Let us see if Elijah is coming to bring him down from the cross!" (Mark 15: 34-37)

Colin McCahon's obsession with Biblical subjects is nowhere more apparent than with his Elias series. He began the paintings in 1959 and altogether painted over 100 works, each one based on the references to Elijah which were made by onlookers to the crucifixion.

He says they emerged out of his reconsideration of the crucifixion, as a result of which he became particularly interested in human doubts. According to McCahon's biographer Gordon Brown, the Elias paintings "are a personal confession in which the artist's concern is less with art than with the meaning of life. It is a confession that, while it affects the solitary person, has been externalized and addressed to all."

Words and colours combine to convey the mood of doubt on the part of the onlookers. "Let be" appears in a cloud and then repeats itself less obviously on the red earth. "Will he" is another of the oft repeated phrases in the whole series. The doubt of the onlookers is expressed in questions: Will Elias (Elijah) come to save? Ever? Never? The struggle of the people goes on and on, the questions never end and the cumulative effect of studying a number of Elias paintings becomes overpowering.

There is the Tau cross of crucifixion in the centre of the painting and the three sections of the painting (a common feature of McCahon's work) reflect the trinity. Small glimpses of light behind the word Elias offer a sign of hope. Faintly discernable at the bottom of the pictures the despondent phrase, "It has always been like this."

The series offers a rare glimpse into the deepest corners of a human heart where hope and despair, faith and uncertainty struggle for supremacy.

Colin McCahon died in New Zealand in 1987. Within a few months of his death he was already being hailed as the greatest artist New Zealand had produced.
Yet during his lifetime he received little recognition and indeed much of his art was ridiculed by the public. In part this was because of the sense of mystery which surrounded his works. Drawing on Christian spirituality and numerology he painted works filled with symbolism which many viewers did not understand. His knowledge of the Bible and of Christian symbols was considerable and influenced his art. In his later years he used words and numbers in profusion and since many of the words came from the apocalyptic writings of the Bible the confusion for some viewers was increased.
At one stage in his life he was attracted to institutional Christianity but never took the step of joining the church.
The Elias work (opposite) was painted in 1959, using Solpah with sand on board. Reproduced with permission of the McCahon family.

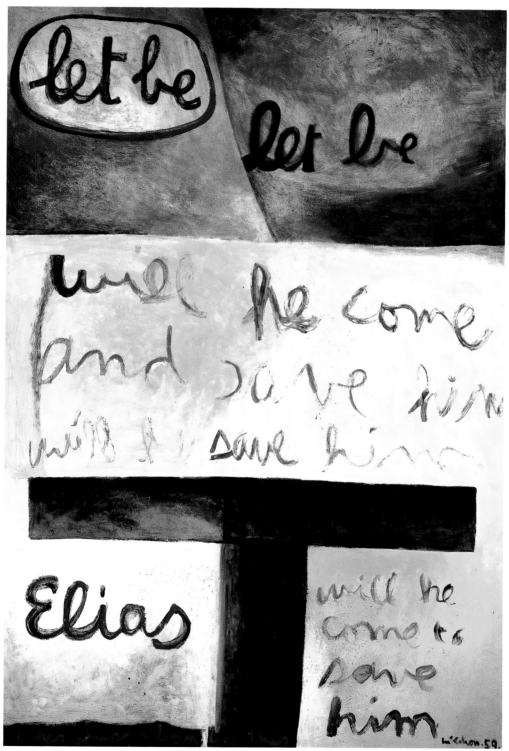

Colin McCahon: Let Be, Let Be

The Death of Jesus

It was about twelve o'clock when the sun stopped shining and darkness covered the whole country until three o'clock; and the curtain hanging in the Temple was torn in two. Jesus cried out in a loud voice, "Father! In your hands I place my spirit!" He said this and died.
(Luke 23: 44-46)

Jesus Christ agonized, brutalized, contorted and distorted, suffers the cross and becomes the symbol of triumph.

Ang argues in his works that human beings are incredible creatures. The figures of Ang are agonized, brutalized, contorted and distorted. They scream, clench their fist, stare at the viewer. People are destroyed but they are not defeated.

In Christ we see the whole suffering of the people concentrated in one person. If it seems too brutal then that is as it should be. The cross is not just for romantics but is the place of realism where all sin and violence come together. We can only bear it because we know that the suffering leads to the victory of God and the triumph of humanity over inhumanity.

Ang Kiukok , born in the Philippines in 1931, is no stranger to suffering. As an evacuee in the mountains of Davao during World War II and as a struggling painter in the slums of Sta Cruz he knew the meaning of poverty.

He discovered Western art late in life and it transformed his own art. When he saw Picasso's Guernica he "felt as if the book of Revelation had been thrown at him."

He began to paint in a radically new way with stark figures of people and animals. The crucifixion which had been a favourite subject for his art now became an emaciated figure of extreme agony and the good church people who had previously enjoyed his art suddenly found the reality of suffering too vivid for their taste.

Kiukok is a quiet man whose simple lifestyle contrasts sharply with his vigorous art but which points to his identification with the suffering of the ordinary people of the Philippines.

Crucifixion

Ang Kiukok: Crucifixion, 1969

Descent from the Cross

Joseph, who was from the town of Arimathea, asked Pilate if he could take Jesus' body (Joseph was a follower of Jesus, but in secret, because he was afraid of the Jewish authorities.) Pilate told him he could have the body, so Joseph went and took it away. Nicodemus, who at first had gone to see Jesus at night, went with Joseph, taking with him about thirty kilogrammes of spices, a mixture of myrrh and aloes. The two men took Jesus' body and wrapped it in linen with the spices according to the Jewish custom of preparing a body for burial. (John 19: 38-40)

Nailed to a cross because you would not
compromise on your convictions.
Nailed to a cross because you would not
bow down before insolent might.
My Saviour, you were laughed at,
derided, bullied, and spat upon
but with unbroken spirit,
Liberator God, you died.

Many young lives are sacrificed
because they will not bend;
many young people in prison
for following your lead.
Daily, you are crucified
my Saviour, you are sacrificed
in prison cells and torture rooms
of cruel and ruthless powers.

The promise of resurrection
the power of hope it holds,
and the vision of a new just order
you proclaimed that first Easter morning.
Therefore, dear Saviour, we can affirm
that although bodies are mutilated and broken,
the spirit refuses submission,
Your voice will never be silenced
Great liberating God.

- Aruna Gnanadason, India

Tadao Tanaka was born in Sapporo, Japan in 1903. The son of a Protestant minister, he studied design at Kyoto Industrial Arts College and later studied painting while working at a Tokyo architect's office.
After World War II he shared in founding the Kodo Art Association and rose to prominence as one of Japan's foremost professional artists, becoming chairman of the board of directors of the Japan Artists' Association.
Since 1950 he has concentrated almost exclusively on Biblical subjects for his art.
Tanaka gave a recent address to Japanese clergy and said: "I do the same work as you." He traced the history of Christian art which "began with illustrations of the Bible, then in the medieval period, art was much utilized for the decoration of churches. In the modern period Christian art has become an art of confessing one's faith." Tanaka adds a fourth purpose - to express the work of salvation in our contemporary context. He argues that "we cannot call artists 'religious artists' just because they treat religious themes. Religious artists are those who respond to contemporary issues through their creativity, coming to grips with real human issues of our times."
His "Descent from the Cross" was painted in oil on canvas, 1965.

Tadao Tanaka: Act of Joseph of Arimathea.

Mary and Jesus

The women who had followed Jesus from Galilee went with Joseph and saw the tomb and how Jesus' body was placed in it. Then they went back home and prepared the spices and perfumes for the body. (Luke 23: 55,56)

"The history of the church in the Philippines is permeated by the presence of Mary. The idea is often premised that for us Filipinos, devotion to Mary is the most striking characteristic that can be said of our Catholic piety. Deep in every Filipino heart and enshrined in every Filipino home is the image of Mary as the object of veneration. Countless shrines to Mary in our country and the throng of devotees who flock to them to pay homage and plead for favours testify to a nation's singular affection for her...

Who is Mary to the Filipino? Mary is *Ang Mahal na Birhen* (the beloved Virgin). She is the model of womanhood whose purity and chastity are worthy of emulation. Being *Ina ng Dios* (Mother of God), relationship with Mary is expressed in petititons for her intercessory powers as an abundant source of merit and help when in trouble.

We have to re-read the scriptures to re-appropriate Mary's role in people's lives today, to re-capture more realistic signs of Mary and discover anew her historical place in a liberating church. The biblical view of Mary would open to us an avenue to the person of Mary as one of our race, so close to us in her refreshing humanity, so clearly identified with our world of conflicts in her understanding and solidarity...

Biblical reflections on the images of Mary point to her as the Jewish woman of witness, unflinching faith and sterling humanity. She is the conscientized and committed Jewish woman who sang in the Mangificat of solidarity in struggle with the poor and the oppressed. Mary is not an impossible model in the Philippine context of injustice today. People who seek a deep commitment in service to the kingdom can draw much inspiration from the Mary of the scriptures." — Hilda Buhay, Philippines

Eduardo Castrillo was born in 1943 in Makati and studied art at the University of Santo Tomas in the Department of Fine Arts. His powerful religious sculptures are landmarks in many parts of the Philippines. A commentator writes: "The jagged lines of Castrillo's work are the genuine expression of his unique personality. The effect comes from his use of diagonal lines rather than vertical. This imbalance is disturbing for some because it communicates restlessness to the viewer."

His "pieta" - Mary holding the body of Jesus - is a feature of the Loyola Memorial Park in Manila.

Eduardo Castrillo: Pieta

Mary weeping

Jesus said to her, "I am the resurrection and the life. Whoever believes in me will live, even though he dies." (John 11: 25)

"The modern history of the Korean people is crowded with stories of death. In the midst of these forces of death - feudal despotism, colonial domination, cruel wars, economic exploitation, and political and military dictatorships in collusion with the great powers - how can we speak of the blessing and promise of life in all its fullness? It sounds paradoxical and illusory. Is it possible to realize life in all its fullness?

For a long time we have been condemned to a pietistic notion of individual salvation and to an other-worldly vision of the Kingdom. But in the course of our struggle in the '70s and '80s we have read the Bible in the concrete context of the suffering of our people. We have rediscovered the meaning of the incarnated God and the resurrection of Jesus Christ. Now we can confidently confess that life overcomes death in the event of Jesus' resurrection and that life is found in the struggles of the people for new life. This conviction has been strengthened during the Kwangju massacre, which is the grimmest tragedy of our modern history.

The Kwangju people's struggle should be understood in connection with the cross of Jesus Christ. The cross is closely intertwined with the resurrection. The cross is the death of God's sacrifical lamb for the redemption of the people.

In Isaiah 53 the suffering servant received the penalties and afflictions for our sins, he lived in miserable and humiliating circumstances and finally became a scapegoat for treason. This suffering is not merely for spiritual redemption but for the total transformation of life - for rebirth.

The vision and promise of life in all its fullness calls the people to march toward peace rather than war; toward wise national self-esteem and cooperation rather than the world powers' struggle for supremacy; toward unification rather than division and toward the paradise of koinonia where all human beings and nature co-exist in justice and peace."

- Korean Student Christian Federation

Taeko Tomiyama was born in Kobe, 1921, and grew up in the Manchuria province of China. The daughter of a businessman, she was sent to the Women's College of Art in Tokyo where she reacted against the narrow confines of a professional artist. A turning point came during labour strikes in 1960 when she was in direct contact with mine workers. She followed the miners to South America to paint aspects of their life and became increasingly identified with third world struggles. "I had no answer for it," she wrote, "until I encountered the student movement in 1970 and finally Kim Chi Ha (the Korean poet) woke me up...I felt as though I had encountered art for the first time."

She began to re-think her role as an artist and refused to sell her work through agents or art galleries. She sets up her own shows, focussing on the suffering of the people.

"What is a painting?" she asks. "Is it a beautiful flower blooming out of a life of affluence? Is it nothing more than a prized possession which is passively admired for its lines or lovely colours? Or does it provoke some sort of human change in those who behold the painting prompting them to action? Does it create the spark that leads to liberation?"

When the occupation of the Korean city of Kwangju by the people was brutally suppressed by the military she painted her "Pieta of Kwangju", one of the best- known images of recent Korean history.

富山妙子 *Tomiyama Taeko*

Taeko Tomiyama: Pieta of Kwangju

The Resurrection

(On finding the empty tomb the women stood puzzled) ... suddenly two men in bright shining clothes stood by them. Full of fear, the women bowed down to the ground, as the men said to them, "Why are you looking among the dead for one who is alive? He is not here; he has been raised." (Luke 24: 4-6a)

> As the seed dies and sprouts again,
> so also with man - Katha Upanishad

> This was the tomb and the aperture
> Through which he came.
> Hope's prayer, most pure.
> He entered the womb unseen,
> giving form to dust,
> then he stole it away -
> the seal on the door
> was unbroken - the flame
> had entered without melting the wax.
> The air, dust laden
> became a figure of light
> as the Word entered the cave,
> stirring the roots of death
> to life!   -Jyoti Sahi, India

The painting of Christ resurrected was dedicated by Korean artist, Hong Chong Myung, during a meeting of the Asian Christian Art Association in Kyoto, 1979. He reflected on its meaning in these words:

"It was raining outside.
I was alone in a foreign city.
Beside the hotel window I stood
and reflected on my country.
What is the destiny of my people?
The people of Korea.
In each of them I see
the mysterious presence of our Lord.

Through the wet glass of the window
His face is seen dimly.
He is being crucified.
There are spots of blood
and his body is bruised.
Even in his suffering
he is the glory of the Risen Lord
Scattered small flowers
Surround him with graceful dew."

Hong Chong Myung paints in a style which reflects his Korean roots. He has sought to reproduce the ochre colours of the earliest cave painters of his land and this unique use of colour makes his paintings easily identifiable.
Born in North Korea in 1922 he studied in Japan and then fled to South Korea before the Chinese invasion. In the chaos of flight one of his daughters was lost and this traumatic event has influenced much of his subsequent art.
Hong Chong Myung is on the executive committee of the Asian Christian Art Association. He is currently President of Soong-Yi College and a widely respected artist in his home country.
The "Risen Lord" (opposite) is painted in oils.

Hong Chong Myung: Risen Lord

Jesus sat down to eat with them, took the bread, and said the blessing; then he broke the bread and gave it to them. Then their eyes were opened and they recognized him, but he disappeared from their sight. They said to each other, "Wasn't it like a fire burning in us when he talked to us on the road and explained the Scriptures to us?"

They got up at once and went back to Jerusalem, where they found the eleven disciples gathered together with the others and saying, "The Lord is risen indeed!" (Luke 24: 30-34a)

In 1985 a small collection of devotional writings was published in China. *Lilies of the Field* by Wang Weifan soon became a popular best-seller and was well-received by educated young Chinese and non-Christian intellectuals. For many Chinese, it provides a spiritually compelling introduction to Christianity. The Easter meditation is called "He is not Here".

"The stone had been rolled away, and our Lord Jesus Christ had risen from the dead. He was no longer in the tomb. Neither the tomb nor death could hold him. The long night is over. The first rays of the morning sun shine across the land. Christ is not in the long night. How could the night hold back the dawn, its morning light breaking through the rosy clouds?

The opaque shadows have been dispersed, the light of the sun plays upon the tomb. Christ is not in the shadows, for shadow and chill cannot swallow warmth and light!

Of what importance are the sighs and weaknesses of yesterday? Christ does not dwell in weakness or defeat. He is the Lord, now strong and victorious, who rose from the dead.

Why wallow in suffering and despair? Christ dwells not in these things, for he is the Lord, confident and hopeful, who rose from the dead.

Why are we rendered helpless by difficulties? Christ does not dwell in our difficulties and inaction, for he is the Lord of life, the Creator who has risen from the dead!"

Lee Myung-Ui was born in Seoul, Korea, October, 1925. At the age of 26 he suffered from tuberculosis and was confined to hospital for the next four years.It was during this time of personal suffering that he became interested in Christianity and at the age of 30 he received baptism.

An early member of the Korean Christian Artists' Association he is director of Hyung Rin Art Academy where he takes a special interest in teaching art to young people.

He is a member of the Hyung Rin Presbyterian Church in Seoul.

In the resurrection painting, Christ appears in the form of a Korean messianic figure.

Lee Myung-Ui: Risen Lord

Doubting Thomas

One of the twelve disciples, Thomas (called the Twin), was not with them when Jesus came. So the other disciples told him, "We have seen the Lord!"
Thomas said to them, "Unless I see the scars of the nails in his hands and put my finger on those scars and my hand in his side, I will not believe."
A week later the disciples were together again indoors, and Thomas was with them. The doors were locked, but Jesus came and stood among them and said, "Peace be with you." Then he said to Thomas, "Put your finger here, and look at my hands; then stretch out your hand and put it in my side. Stop your doubting, and believe!"
Thomas answered him, "My Lord and my God!" (John 20: 24-28)

When he was a child, Michael Smither was taught that doubt was a sinful and negative trait but, despite this, he always had a sneaking respect for Thomas as a person who had the strength to stand alone and make a personal search for the truth. When asked to paint a church mural, he chose Thomas because, he said, "he was, for me, one of the most courageous of the apostles. He had to find out for himself. It was a courageous thing to do. I named one of my children Thomas."

Michael Smither is an artist formed by powerful forces. One of these is a deep compassion for the land. In the past he has taken part in many crusades to improve the environment and now he is living in an isolated area of Taranaki, New Zealand in a small house without electricity where he paints and reflects on life. His house is on 25 acres of land which he is attempting to restore to native forest.
Another strong force in his life has been his religious faith, learned in Catholic schools. Although he is no longer a practising Catholic, his art reflects his search for a spiritual meaning to life.
St Francis is his favourite saint and the subject of one of his best-known works.
He was commissioned to prepare 14 Stations of the Cross for St Joseph's Church in New Plymouth, New Zealand and although there was controversy because parishioners thought they were too stark, he was, nevertheless, later invited to paint a mural on the back wall of the church.
He has completed the mural of "Doubting Thomas" (opposite) and is now painting a second mural on the baptism of Jesus.

Doubting Thomas (Detail)

Michael Smither: Doubting Thomas - Mural

Jesus Commissions the Disciples

Jesus drew near and said to them, "I have been given all authority in heaven and on earth. Go, then, to all peoples everywhere and make them my disciples: baptize them in the name of the Father, the Son, and the Holy Spirit, and teach them to obey everything I have commanded you. And I will be with you always, to the end of the age." (Matthew 28: 18-20)

"A problem in making the Great Commission the basis of Christian mission is that all kinds of people without either the right or the spiritual candour to give witness set themselves up as persons who have been commanded to give witness. Here witness becomes counter-witness...

The Bible, by and large, talks about believers, not about converts. In Jesus' own ministry, people did not have to move from one community to another, but from a self-centred life to a God-centred life. Repentance has to do with a radical renewal of relationship with God and one's neighbours...

It is of course true that a number of persons took up discipleship, called themselves by his name, and after the resurrection the church became a historical reality. But can we say that the gospel message or the fact that believers became an identifiable community provides a Biblical basis to speak of others as 'unreached millions?' 'Unreached by whom?' asks Stanley Samartha in one of his essays. The fact that the preacher has not reached a place or spoken to a people does not mean that God has not reached them."

- Wesley Ariarajah, Sri Lanka

"Christ is the first-born of all creation, the head of all created reality. He loves not only all men and women, but also all that is created. I am united to Christ in baptism and confirmation. My mind is the mind of Christ. Therefore my love is non-exclusive and open to the whole creation. Nothing is alien or threatening. Love and compassion for the whole creation is the characteristic of Christ. The church as his body shares in this love and compassion. I, as a member of that body, have to express that love and compassion in faithfulness, integrity and openness, with sympathetic understanding. This is sufficient and compelling reason for me to engage in dialogue with people of other faiths. It is love in Christ that sends me to dialogue."

- Paulos Mar Gregorius, India

Shin Young-Hun was born in Pyoungnam, North Korea in 1923. He studied at the Teachers' Training College in Pyongyang and the Seoul Art Academy. His life since then has been spent teaching at art schools and painting.

As a child he went to a Catholic Church and when he was in Seoul in 1955 he was baptized in a Presbyterian church. He has always had a lively interest in the Bible and takes his themes from aspects of the Bible which interest him.

Since 1966 he has been a member of the Korean Christian Artists' Association.

Shin is a surrealist artist and his striking art works, drawn from his faith, deal with human loneliness, alienation, and the struggle of modern life.

Shin Young-Hun: Outreach of the New Covenant

The Ascension of Jesus

(Jesus said to the disciples) "When the Holy Spirit comes upon you, you will be filled with power, and you will be witnesses for me in Jerusalem, in all Judaea and Samaria, and to the ends of the earth." After saying this, he was taken up to heaven as they watched him and a cloud hid him from their sight. (Acts 1: 8,9)

"Hindu India developed a magnificent image to describe God's relationship with creation. God 'dances' creation. God is the dancer, creation is his dance. The dance is different from the dancer yet it has no existence apart from him. You cannot take it home in a box. The moment the dancer stops, the dance ceases to be.

In our quest for God, we think too much, reflect too much, talk too much. Even when we look at the dance we call creation, we are all the time thinking, talking (to ourselves and others), reflecting, analysing, philosophysing. Words. Noise.

Be silent and contemplate the Dance. Just look. A star, a flower, a fading leaf, a bird, a stone - any fragment of the Dance will do. And hopefully, it won't be long before you see the Dancer!"

- Anthony de Mello, India

Let the links of my shackles snap at every step
    of thy dance,
      O Lord of Dancing,
and let my heart wake in the freedom of the
    eternal voice.
Let it feel the touch of that foot that ever sets
    swinging the lotus-seat of the muse,
and with its perfume maddens the air
    through ages.
Rebellious atoms are subdued into forms at
    thy dance time,
the suns and planets - anklets of light - twirl round
    thy moving feet,
and, age after age, things struggle to wake from
    dark slumber, through pain of life
    into consciousness,
and the ocean of thy bliss breaks out into tumults
    of suffering and joy.

- Rabindranath Tagore, India

Bagong Kussudiardja was born in 1928 in Indonesia and brought up among artists. He began to study the classical dances of Java at the age of 18 and his love of dance has always been foremost in his life. After independence in 1945, Bagong began to experiment with dances which would reflect the new spirit in Indonesia. Always creative and innovative, he had many critics but just as many supporters.

He wrote: "Art is a part of my life. I feel that one needs art just as one needs food, clothing and shelter. I live every day receptive to everything surrounding me, open to the past and the things inherited from my ancestors, the present and the future. Even though something may be very small, I try to understand it completely, since human life must be able to appreciate the vitality of all things."

Bagong takes a close interest in all aspects of the arts. He is a skilled batik painter and as the painting opposite indicates, his oil paintings also rank with the finest. His painting of the dancing Christ ascending to heaven was prepared for the Second Conference of the Asian Christian Art Association held in the Philippines.

Bagong currently heads a dance training centre and an education institute in Yogyakarta, Indonesia.

Bagong Kussudiardja: The Ascension

The Day of Pentecost

When the day of Pentecost came, all the believers were gathered together in one place. Suddenly there was a noise from the sky which sounded like a strong wind blowing, and it filled the whole house where they were sitting. Then they saw what looked like tongues of fire which spread out and touched each person there. They were all filled with the Holy Spirit and began to talk in other languages, as the Spirit enabled them to speak. (Acts 2: 1-4)

The Spirit was poured out on the believers in Jerusalem in the form of a flame. It is an image which is readily understood in Asian societies where indigenous religions use the flame as a symbol of purification and the cleansing power of God.

The flame is often stylized in the shape of a bodhi leaf since the bodhi tree is the sacred tree under which the Buddha received enlightenment. A similar shape is seen in the work of Indian artists Paul Koli (page 40) and Jyoti Sahi (page 130).

In this Thai portrayal of Pentecost (opposite) a curtain marks off the space in which the disciples met as a family. The artist introduces a nice touch by reminding us that children were present at Pentecost and the Holy Spirit came to them as well. The clothing of the people shows that those of both high-class and low-class society received the flame of the Spirit.

In Thai mythology, red is the colour of heaven and the strong use of red in the painting is the reminder that heaven came to the people at Pentecost.

"I want to pay a simple tribute to God the Holy Spirit. The Spirit, the *ruha elohim* is feminine gender in the Old Testament, neuter in the New Testament, but never masculine.

It operates quietly - sometimes it comes with a mighty roaring wind and thunder and lightning. That is exceptional. Most of the time, it works quietly and is at work in the churches of Asia, in the societies of Asia, in the whole global development.

In my church, the liturgy every Sunday speaks of the Holy Spirit who brings all things that exist, and all the things which are to exist in the future, to perfection. That is the job of the Spirit: to bring everything to perfection. The Spirit is quietly at work. Would that we have the sensitivity to see where it is at work and become available, so that we can truly become the instruments of the Spirit. That is the commitment I hope all of us have." - Paulos Mar Gregorius, India

Sawai Chinnawong was born in Thailand in 1959. He grew up in the Buddhist tradition and it was the enjoyment of Buddhist paintings which made him determined to become an artist. During High School he converted to Christianity. After studying art at the Taiwichitsin Institute in Bangkok he entered the McGilvray Faculty of Theology at Payap University, Chiengmai where he graduated with arts and theology degrees in 1989. Since then he has been part of the Church Arts program of the Church of Christ in Thailand. This innovative program funds indigenous Christian art in Thailand and encourages its use in churches. Sawai is the first Resident Artist in this program. His paintings use traditional Thai art forms and images to convey the Christian message in a way local people will understand.

Sawai Chinnawong: Pentecost

The Community of Believers

All the believers continued together in close fellowship and shared their belongings with one another. They would sell their property and possessions, and distribute the money among all, according to what each one needed. (Acts 2: 44,45)

"When I read the gospels, I read them as an Aboriginal. There are many things in the gospel that make me happy to be an Aboriginal, because I think we have a good start.

So many of the things Christ said and did, and the way he lived, make me think of the good things in our way of life. Christ did not get worried over material things. In fact he looked down on them as things that get in the way and make it hard to get to our true country.

He was born in the countryside in a cave, like many of us have been born. He walked about like us and with nowhere to lay his head. He died with nothing, on a cross. So many of our people died with nothing. He had his own little group like us. He was strong on sharing - 'if someone wants your tunic, give him your cloak.' We do a lot of things like that. Of course he went a lot further: in the eucharist, he shared himself as nobody else could.

Like him we have a deep sense of God in nature. We like the way he used the things of nature to teach and the important part nature plays in the sacraments.

We find it easy to see in Christ **the** great Dreamtime figure who, more than all others, gave us law and ceremony and life centres and marked out the way we must follow to reach our true country.

So it is not over-difficult to realise that Christ is with us always. We do not find it strange when he says he is the life, that we can and must live with his life, that in this life of his we are one. He lives in us and is us, so that when we do for each other, we do for him."

- Deacon Boniface Perdjert, Australian Aboriginal

Kaapa Mbitjinpa Tjampitjinpa is an Australian Aboriginal: a member of the Anmatjera tribe. A member of the Pupunya desert artists' group, his work is eagerly sought by collectors. A stickler for traditional protocols his skill in the new acrylic medium brought him national fame. In recent years his eyesight has declined and he can only paint for short periods. Like all aboriginal art his work is full of religious symbolism and meaning. In the "Soakage Site" (opposite) the tribal community sit together around a central site.

Kaapa Tjampitjinpa: The Soakage Pit

Paul the Missionary

When day came, the sailors did not recognize the coast, but they noticed a bay with a beach and decided that, if possible, they would run the ship aground there. So they cut off the anchors and let them sink in the sea, and at the same time they untied the ropes that held the steering oars. Then they raised the sail at the front of the ship so that the wind would blow the ship forward, and we headed for shore. But the ship hit a sandbank and went aground. (Acts 27: 39-41a)

Paul did not want the ship to sail from the port of Fair Haven but the centurion in charge of the ship refused to listen to him.

"Those in charge of the affairs of the world see no reason why they should listen to the counsels of the church. How often the prophets of the Old Testament were in this situation! Statescraft demanded an alliance with Egypt, but the prophet advised against it. National honour demanded rebellion, but the prophet counselled submission. War demanded stern measures, but the prophet pleaded for mercy. Military weakness demanded compromise but the prophet advocated resistance. Is it any wonder that, so persistently, we are told the church must keep out of politics! It is one thing, the men of the world say, for the church to enunciate general principles, it is another thing for the church to speak specifically with respect to any situation...

The climax of the story came when the ship ran aground and the passengers were able to swim ashore. The soldiers, afraid that some of the prisoners might swim to freedom, wanted to kill them. But the centurion, wishing to save Paul, kept them from carrying out their purpose. This is a touching story. How literally the promise was fulfilled that Paul's fellow-prisoners were saved because of him...

It is a serious responsibility when people, whether enemy or friend, stranger or neighbour, in want or in wealth, in distress or despair, are committed into our hands. But the situation itself is inescapable. To be bound to the secular is to be bound to other people. To serve the Lord is to serve those for whom he died."

- D.T. Niles, Sri Lanka

Sister Claire is a Catholic nun working among the poor in Bangalore. Her life reads like a novel. Born of orthodox Hindu parents and the eldest of nine children, she wanted to become a sanyasini - one who retreats from the world in search of enlightenment, but at a convent school she was attracted to some aspects of Christianity, especially Christ's humility and silence. At the age of 16 her parents arranged for her marriage but rather than go through with it she ran away from home and after some adventures joined a Catholic convent. Her parents traced her and tried to make her return. She refused and they parted in anger. Alienation from her parents caused a breakdown. Not until she was near to death did a reconciliation with her parents take place and they converted to Christianity.

Claire's Mother Superior encouraged her to take up art as a means of therapy and she soon discovered a hidden talent.

She joined Sr Genevieve to paint 140 art works of the Bible (see p.52). The shipwreck of Paul at sea (opposite) is one of them. Painted in folk-art style her paintings have a popular appeal in India.

Sister Claire: Shipwreck

Love

Love is eternal. There are inspired messages, but they are temporary; there are gifts of speaking in strange tongues, but they will cease; there is knowledge, but it will pass. For our gifts of knowledge and of inspired messages are only partial; but when what is perfect comes, then what is partial will disappear...
Meanwhile these three remain: faith, hope, and love; and the greatest of these is love.
(1 Corinthians 13: 8-10,13)

Can there be a love which does not make demands on those who are the objects of love?
- K'ung Fu-tse, China

Love is the strongest force the world possesses and yet it is the humblest imaginable.

The more efficient a force is, the more silent and subtle it is. Love is the subtlest force in the world.
- M. Gandhi, India

We cannot love only our own race. We need to have a more encompassing goal - to love the world, peoples of all the world. For all humankind is created by God. If we love only our own race this is the kind of narrow racism which can undermine and destroy world peace. We want to love all humankind. This is a holy mission given to every Christian. - C.M. Kao, Taiwan

There are three kinds of love - unselfish, mutual and selfish. Unselfish love is the highest kind. The lover only cares for the welfare of the beloved and ignores their own sufferings. In mutual love the lover not only wants the happiness of the beloved but has an eye toward their own happiness as well. It is in the middle. Selfish love is the lowest. It looks only to its own happiness no matter whether the beloved suffers as a consequence. - Sri Ramakrishna

Yoon Young Ja is one of Korea's handful of pioneer modern sculptors. She is the only woman in this select company.
In 1950 it was hard to make a living as a sculptor and even more difficult to establish a place for oneself in the art world but she has succeeded and is now regarded as one of the country's top sculptors.
As a woman artist, the archetypal images of femaleness and motherhood have dominated her art. Korean commentator, Oh Kwang-su has written of her work: "A strong feeling for life pervades her work. It is based on the structure of the human body, conveying her sense of humanity in her choice of symbolic shapes. Her current works are planted in the earth but escalate into space, a harmony of vitality and sensitivity."
She is currently President of the Korean Christian Artists' Association.
Her sculpture Love-1 (opposite) measures 135x114x42cms.

Yoon Young Ja: Love-1, 1985

Crucified with Christ

So far as the Law is concerned, however, I am dead - killed by the Law itself - in order that I might live for God. I have been put to death with Christ on his cross, so that it is no longer I who live, but it is Christ who lives in me. This life that I live now, I live by faith in the Son of God, who loved me and gave his life for me. (Galatians 2: 19,20)

When Kim Yong Gil was a school teacher in Korea, there was one student who was causing many problems around the school. He made trouble for the teachers in class as well as for the other students. Nobody took him seriously and he had no real friends among the pupils.

One day Kim invited him to come to his studio. It was a cold winter day but even so, he asked the boy to remove his shoes and socks. Kim painted the sole of the boy's foot with black paint and pressed it onto a clean sheet of paper. He did the same with the other foot and then made further prints with both his right and left hands.

After some days, Kim went to his class and showed them the completed work (opposite). He explained how it had been done and then announced the name of the boy who had provided the prints. The boy himself became more popular with the class after this event and he seemed to change his whole approach to life.

The text of Paul - "I am crucified with Christ" was visible in a very literal way every time he saw the painting.

Later, the student spoke of that event as the turning point in his life and the beginning of his Christian experience.

Kim Yong Gil is a Korean artist who has developed a distinctive way of painting which has proved very popular with church groups in Korea and America.

Currently he is Professor of Art at Pusan National University but his real vocation seems dedicated to the development of a World Christian Art Museum of which he is the Director. The Museum was opened in 1988 at Young-do, Pusan, Korea and has attracted wide interest. A feature of the museum is to be the world's largest Christian art work which, when completed, will be 100x100 metres in size.

His painting (opposite) is done with Indian ink and colouring on rice paper.

Kim Yong Gil: Crucifixion

Freedom

Freedom is what we have - Christ has set us free! Stand, then, as free people, and do not allow yourselves to become slaves again. (Galatians 5: 1)

We raise our eyes in prayer
through the bars, darkly.

Together with a thousand prisoners in their cells
and with many more thousands in the larger
prison of our country.

We pray for freedom
and even more urgently, for life.

As nameless executioners salvage
those whom they used to merely torture and detain
and both children and parents
slowly but surely die
of sickness that has many names
and only one name.

We ask for faith
to see that death and prison are not forever
that life and freedom will prevail.

We ask for faith
to celebrate even while we mourn
knowing that death and prison
are already signs of a people's struggle
for freedom and life.

We raise our voices in prayer
through the bars, boldly
believing there will be an answer
as our people awaken.

Amen.

     - Edicio de la Torre, 1984

Fr Edicio de la Torre, a Catholic priest of the Society of the Divine Word, was born in the Philippines in 1943.

During the Marcos years, while teaching theology and sociology at the Seminary, he became directly involved in movements for social change including the post of national chaplain for the Federation of Free Farmers. When martial law was declared he went underground but was captured and imprisoned in 1974. There was no trial and after more than five years he was released in 1980 for studies in Rome. He returned after two years and was again arrested.

Following the people's revolution in 1986, he was released and has since left the order and is living in Europe.

During his time in prison he wrote meditations and poetry and developed his skills at painting.

A charismatic leader, Father Ed' never lost touch with the poor and marginalised people of his country. His fierce concern for justice is evident in all his artistic expressions.

One of his favourite themes was "Freedom" and the painting in oils (opposite) is typical of his style.

Edicio de la Torre: Kalayaan (Freedom)

Christis our Peace

For Christ himself has brought us peace by making Jews and Gentiles one people. With his own body he broke down the wall that separated them and kept them enemies. He abolished the Jewish Law with its commandments and rules, in order to create out of the two races one new people in union with himself, in this way making peace. (Ephesians 2: 14,15)

"Peace, in the Biblical sense of 'Shalom' means wholeness. The blessing, 'peace to you', is a prayer and promise of wholeness and well-being which can be a human experience because of the 'grace and mercy' of God.

In the Bible, peace is the fruit or effect of righteousness (Isa 32:15). God's righteousness is a committed and liberating relationship with humanity, and our committed and liberating relationship with others constitutes our righteousness. Justice is the action which expresses that relationship and creates peace. Peace and justice are mutually interdependent and inseparable...

Because peace means 'wholeness', it refers to the overcoming of division and conflict wherever domination and hostility reign. Paul said, in relation to the conflict of Jewish and Gentile Christians, 'Christ is our peace, who has made us both one, and has broken down the dividing wall of hostility.'

In Asia today there are conflicts between nations and between groups within nations, wherever one would dominate the other - between social and economic classes, between religious groups, between ethnic minorities and the prevailing society. All are issues of peace and justice.

Conflicts are not for mere conflict resolution with whatever compromise and appeasement may be necessary. Peace is not mere absence of conflict, but the removal of the causes of conflict. Peace is not a new acquiescence in the status quo but a new community life based on the righting of wrongs."

- Harvey Perkins, Australia

Jonathon T. Carpio is an art student in Manila. At the Ninth Assembly of the Christian Conference in Asia, held June 1990, he won first prize in a competition for an art work to illustrate the assembly theme, "Christ our Peace".

In his acrylic painting (opposite) he picks up the theme of the text, that Christ has made all one, by showing tribal people from different parts of the Philippines coming together through the power of God's spirit. The painting is owned by the National Council of Churches in the Philippines.

Jonathon T. Carpio: Christ Our Peace

The Humility of Christ

Of his own free will he (Christ Jesus) gave up all that he had,
    and took the form of a servant.
He became like man
    and appeared in human likeness.
He was humble and walked the path of obedience all the way to death -
    his death on the cross...   (Philippians 2: 7,8)

"The God whom we adore, follow and have faith in, walked this earth as a human being, Jesus Christ. This immortal and omnipotent God was incarnate on earth as the son of an unwed mother, a scandal which would have made Joseph and Mary the target of insidious ridicule.

Jesus lived a simple life and moved among the poor and downtrodden, the drunkards, prostitutes, tax-gatherers, women, lepers, the sick and the Samaritans. He shared the lot of the people of Israel: a people subjugated by a foreign power. He chose as his close associates the fishermen, women and workers. In the Graeco-Roman empire, as in some societies today, women were considered non-persons but Jesus befriended them so that Mary and Martha of Bethany and Mary Magdalene were among his close associates. He lived among the people he loved and to them he revealed his true identity.

In the Garden of Gethsemane, Christ prayed that 'the cup would pass from him.' He knew what lay ahead of him, but was willing to humble himself and be killed as a common criminal on the cross so that God's purpose could be fulfilled.

In Jesus Christ, God humbled Godself and died on a cross so that we might live. Are we willing to humble ourselves with Jesus Christ forgetting our claims to fame, wealth and security ready to 'die to ourselves' so that the down-trodden in our societies may live?"

          - Annathaie Abayasekera, Sri Lanka

Nyoman Darsane was born in the Balinese village of Pajangan in 1939.

His father was a musician and his grandfather a dancer and Darsane inherited the family's artistic tradition.

He studied at the Institute of Teachers School for Fine Arts in Jakarta where he was greatly influenced by the work of Vincent Van Gogh and Gauguin.

In 1966 he was baptized and has been an active proponent of the Christian faith through the arts. In addition to his main work as an artist, he is an accomplished dancer and musician.

His painting of the dancing Christ was painted in oils in 1978 for the first consultation of the Asian Christian Art Association. It portrays the humility of Christ coming into human experience and sharing the life of the people. The worshipper prays with a flower between her fingers in an attitude common to the people of Bali.

Nyoman Darsane: He Came Down

... For this reason God raised him to the highest place above
and gave him the name that is greater than any other name.
And so, in honour of the name of Jesus
all beings in heaven, on earth, and in the world below
will fall on their knees,
and all will openly proclaim that Jesus Christ is Lord,
to the glory of God the Father. (Philippians 2: 9-11)

"The conditions for 'greatness' are seen in the human life of Jesus of Nazareth.

His self-emptying ('kenosis') is truly astounding. He is revealed in the gospels as being at the lowest points of human existence: born among cattle in a stable and dying as a seditionist and agitator with two criminals outside the city wall.

In all this, his obedience to God was a loving unto death - a life spent in loving and in complete solidarity with people. It was a life spent in humble service in which Jesus was identified with the poorest, the lowliest and the lost. Therefore, he became a threat to the authorities and suffered political oppression to the point of torture and death on a cross.

It is the crucified love of Christ, living and dying for others that is the essence of his greatness.

Such crucified love must necessarily be eternal. The name and character and life of Jesus will be the magnet which will draw all people to Jesus Christ as Lord.

Our elder brother Jesus has taken our vulnerable crucified humanity with the scars of his own wounds into the very heart of God. Hence, 'Jesus is Lord' is the hopeful cry on the lips of everyone who strives for total liberation. The greatness of Jesus Christ is precisely his servanthood and solidarity with the broken victims of the principalities and powers of our day and age, as of all ages.

Jesus reigns and saves from his cross in the aching heart of God."   - Jeffrey Abayasekera, Sri Lanka

Hendrato is a Javanese artist from Indonesia. He uses a batik technique for his paintings and the figures are steeped in traditional Javanese symbols and imagery.
He is a recent convert to Christianity, having been baptized in 1982.

Hendrato: God Exalted

Light and Life

Now the message that we have heard from his Son and announce is this: God is light, and there is no darkness at all in him. If, then, we say that we have fellowship with him, yet at the same time live in the darkness, we are lying both in our words and in our actions. But if we live in the light - just as he is in the light - then we have fellowship with one another, and the blood of Jesus, his Son, purifies us from every sin. (1 John 1: 5-7)

Indian ashrams have always been places for reflection on spirituality. In Christian ashrams there has been a particular affection for the gospel and letters of John and these writings are often compared with the teaching of the Upanishads, the Hindu texts written around 650 B.C.
One of the best-known quotations from the Upanishads is the prayer:

> From untruth lead me to truth,
> From darkness lead me to light,
> From death lead me to life.

Each of the three prayers - for truth, light and life - are answered in the Johannine writings by the affirmations of Jesus:

> I am the way, the truth and the life (John 14: 6).
> I am the light of the world (John 8: 12).
> I am the resurrection and the life (John 11: 21).

According to Swami Abhishiktananda this "experience of the self, as we say in India, is the highest possible attainment of human beings."

Jin Song-Ja was born in 1945. She graduated from the Department of Sculpture at the College of Fine Arts, Seoul University. She has won several prizes at the National Arts exhibition and is a lecturer at Dong-Duk Women's College.
She has recently expanded her focus by dealing with a number of religious themes and describes her life as a quest for "holy songs". She believes that sculpture is a medium which can express her way of life. So for her, to "sing a holy song" is the same as doing sculpture.
A love of holiness is at the heart of her sculpture.

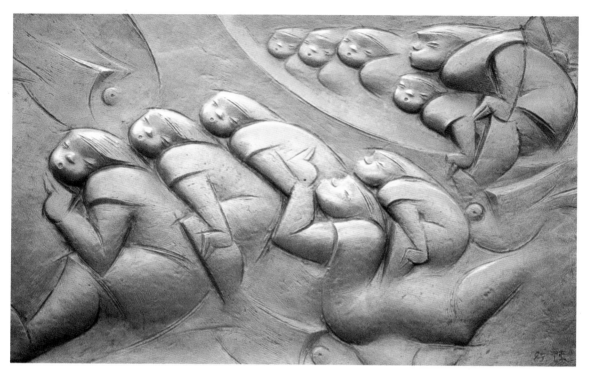

Jin Song-Ja: Light and Life

The City of God

The Spirit took control of me, and the angel carried me to the top of a very high mountain. He showed me Jerusalem, the Holy City, coming down out of heaven from God and shining with the glory of God. The city shone like a precious stone, like a jasper, clear as crystal... I did not see a temple in the city, because its temple is the Lord God Almighty and the Lamb. The city has no need of the sun or the moon to shine on it, because the glory of God shines on it, and the Lamb is its lamp.(Revelation 21: 10,11,22,23)

"The Kingdom of God does not exist because of your effort or mine. It exists because God reigns. Our part is to enter this kingdom and bring our life under God's sovereign will." — T.Z. Koo, China

Korean artist Yi Choon-Ki gives an interpretation of the holy city which will scarcely be recognisable to Western eyes, but whose symbolism will immediately be understood by persons from North Asia who are in tune with their own traditions.

The perfect city of Korea is based on the ancient living space - square and protected from all sides. The yellow earth in the centre is a reminder of the roots of society. On each of the four sides the whole cosmos is summarised. In terms of the compass: East is blue; West is white; South is red and North is black. The whole of creation is also symbolised with the blue dragon, white tiger, red sparrow and black reptile. Finally, the colours represent the rhythm of the seasons: spring is blue (and from the east); autumn or fall is white; summer is red; and winter is black.

These colours are still used at ceremonial events to sum up the perfect wholeness of creation. Banners of each colour hang behind the four corners of the Sumo wrestler's mat.

Above the perfect city, the holy city of God, stands the light - the light of the sun or of the Son.

Yi Choon-Ki was born in 1933 in Seoul, Korea. He graduated from the College of Fine Arts, Seoul National University in 1960. He is currently Professor of Painting in the college of Fine Arts at Chonju University.

He is a prolific painter whose work is well-known in exhibitions in Korea, and more recently abroad. In 1989-90 he was the Visiting Artist at Towson State University, USA. "Work 86" (opposite) is one of a series of oil paintings on cosmology.

Yi Choon-Ki: Work '86

The Tree of Life

"Listen!" says Jesus. "I am coming soon! I will bring my rewards with me, to give to each one according to what he has done. I am the first and the last, the beginning and the end." Happy are those who wash their robes clean and so have the right to eat the fruit from the tree of life and to go through the gates into the city. (Revelation 22: 12-14)

"You will find Chinese Christians talking not only about the Redeemer Christ, but more now about the Cosmic Christ, the Incarnational Christ, Christ as the crown and fulfilment of the whole creative process, the clue to creation, the one whom we find talked about in the New Testament, especially in the fourth gospel, in Colossians and in Ephesians. And in this way we think that many contemporary thoughts and movements are not in contrast with the divine revelation or destructive of divine revelation, but rather means of illuminating that revelation. They are not adversaries but glimpses and foreshadows of the way of Christ. In looking at reality this way, we think we are not diminishing the unique significance of Christ but are magnifying his glory and confirming his claims.

We are deeply impressed by the fact that Christ showed very meagre interest in specially sacred doings. We are impressed by his profound interest in the most ordinary doings of secular life. He was interested in lilies and birds, the sower and seeds, in women and children, in a father with two sons, in the fishermen, in baking of bread by the housewife, in the merchant seeking pearls. He didn't aim at turning us away from the natural order and from the world, but used them to enable us to discover in them manifestations of truth about God.

Now a world which can be used so often to teach us about God cannot be an entirely fallen one.

...We discover the immanence of the transcendent God in history, in nature, in the people's movements and in the collectivities in which we find ourselves. After all, the God who is worthy of our worship and praise is not so small as to be concerned only with a few million Chinese who profess to believe in him. God's love and care is for the whole of humanity."

- K.H. Ting, China

Brother Joseph McNally is a Malaysian citizen living in Singapore. Born in Ireland in 1923 he received a doctor's degree in Fine Art at Colombia University in 1968. Most of his life has been spent in South-East Asia.

He taught at St Patrick's College, Singapore for many years and made a unique contribution to the development of education in newly-independent Singapore.

He has now become Principal of La Salle Art School which is attached to St Patrick's and there he continues to help students develop their talents in the field of art.

As a sculptor, Joseph McNally has often been recognized with commissions for art work in churches. He makes use of scrap metal in many of his sculpture works, especially favouring car bumper bars. His work, "Christ the Tree of Life" is welded from found metal.

Joseph McNally: The Tree of Life

Do Not Harm the Earth

After this I saw four angels standing at the four corners of the earth, holding back the four winds so that no wind should blow on the earth or the sea or against any tree. And I saw another angel coming up from the east with the seal of the living God. He called out in a loud voice to the four angels to whom God had given the power to damage the earth and the sea. The angel said, "Do not harm the earth, the sea, or the trees, until we mark the servants of our God with a seal on their foreheads." (Revelation 7: 1-3)

Japanese artist Sadao Watanabe spends much time reading the Bible to draw inspiration for his art. He found a surprising and contemporary message when he began to read the book of Revelation.

"I understood the angels trying to hold back the winds," he said. "We in Japan also have our Gods of the winds who control the cosmos."

So he painted the world with the angels controlling the winds and there in the middle were all the people of the world on their earthly journey - men, women and children. Some are injured and others have their crosses broken but all have the hope that they will have a new seal on their foreheads.

Meanwhile the message of the angels is clear: Do not harm the earth, the sea or the trees. It is a timely call to humankind on the edge of the twenty-first century.

Do not harm the earth
Live in harmony with all creation
Let the waters flow pure
The trees grow straight and tall

Show justice and mercy to all
And pray for a land of peace
Respect all living creatures
Love and adore the Lord

Then shall the mountains sing for joy
The flowers of the field dance in praise
All people shall live together in unity
And all shall be well with the earth.

Sadao Watanabe of Japan, is one of Asia's best-known Christian artists. His works are found in collections from the Vatican museum to the White House in Washington. His distinctive graphic style makes the prints particularly useful for illustration and a Watanabe art work will often be seen on the cover of a book or as a poster.

Born in 1913, Watanabe converted to Christianity in 1930 and eventually found his vocation as a stencil printer of Biblical subjects. He developed a unique technique based on a traditional Okinawan craft. His works are printed on hand-made washi paper and have an icon-like quality which makes them universally popular.

Throughout his career he has painted almost 400 works - all on Biblical themes. Some of these themes have so impressed him that he has painted them several times. "Noahs' Ark" has appeared in 11 different versions and the "Lord's Supper" has been painted 20 times. One of his more recent works on the Lord's supper appears on the cover of this book.

We have chosen a particularly interesting Watanabe from a lesser-known Biblical passage to complete this collection of Asian art.

Sadao Watanabe: The Angel Ascends from the Rising of the Sun

Acknowledgements

The editors acknowledge the support of many people in publishing the text of this book. The following page listing refers to pages in this book. In the selection of meditations to accompany the art works there has been extensive use of ecumenical writings.

From World Council of Churches Publications: p.7 Masao Takenaka,*God is Rice*, Risk Book Series,1986; p.30 T.K. Thomas,"Meditation",*One World*, May 1988; p.80 Marianne Katoppo,*Compassionate and Free*, Risk Book Series, 1979; p.162 Wesley Ariarajah,*The Bible and People of Other Faiths*,Risk Book Series,1985; p.145 D.T. Niles,"Prayer",*For All God's People - Ecumenical Prayer Cycle*, 1978.

From publications of the Christian Conference of Asia: p.18 Chuan Su-Jen,"The New Mission of Asian Christians",*CTC Bulletin*, April 1990, and p.26 ibid Rosemary Russell,"Seedtime and Harvest"; p.32 George Ninan,"Bible Study",*Minutes of the URM Meeting*, Taiwan, 1989; p.46 Chitra Fernando,"Women and Racism",*Reading the Bible as Asian Women*,(Women's Desk) 1986; p.52 Marianne Katoppo,"Bible Study",*Towards a Theological Basis for Education*,(Asian Ecumenical Course) 1982; p.54 Wesley Ariarajah,"Reflection",*An Asian Theological Reflection on Suffering and Hope*, 1977; p.64 and p.76 *Sound the Bamboo - CCA Hymnal* Hymn 71:Wefan Wang,"Winter has Passed",tr. and copyright Ewing W. Carroll Jr.,Music: Shengben Lin,arr. Pen-li Chen and Hymn 144:Shirley Murray,"Hunger Carol", Music: I-to Loh; p.66 Rienzie Perera, "Bible Study",*Christ Our Peace*,*Ninth CCA Assembly*, Manila, 1990; p.68 James K. Baxter, "Song of the Holy Spirit" and p.108 ibid, W.S. Rendra,"Poem of an Angry Man",*Your Will be Done*, (Youth Desk) 1984; p.96 ,"Bible Study", Prakai Nontawasee and p.104 Huang Po Ho,"Bible Study",*Asia Mission Conference*, 1989; p.120 Lakshman Wickremesinghe, "Address",*CCA Seventh Assembly*, Bangalore, 1981; p.120 D. Preman Niles, *Towards the Sovereignty of People*, ,(Theological Desk) 1983; p.124 Park Sang Jung,"Your Kingdom Come",*CTC Bulletin*, January-April, 1986; p.140, *No Place in the Inn-Voices of Minority People in Asia*,(Urban Rural Mission) 1979; p.162 Paulos Mar Gregorius,"Dimensions of our Asian Captivity",*Minutes of Eighth CCA Assembly*,Seoul, 1985; p.178, Harvey Perkins,"Section Report",*Ninth CCA Assembly*, Manila, 1990.

Image is the quarterly magazine of the Asian Christian Art Association. It contains further information on many of the artists in this book. Direct quotations used in this book are: p.8 Jyoti Sahi, *Image 20*, 1984; p.38 Jyoti Sahi, *Image 38*, 1989; p.188 K.H. Ting, *Image 16*, 1983.

Other publications from which quotations are used include: p.12 He Qi,"On the Appreciation of Christian Art",*Chinese Theological Review*, 1986; p.36 and p.60 C.S. Song,*Tell us Your Name*, Orbis Press, NY, 1964; p.42 Sang-Chul Lee and Erich Weingartner, *The Wanderer, Autobiography of a United Church Moderator*, Wood Lake Books, Canada, 1989; p.82 Karl Gasper,*How Long*, Clarentian Publications, Manila; p.88 Douglas McKenzie, *The Mango Tree Church*, Joint Board of Christian Education, Melbourne, 1988; p.90 D.T. Niles, *For Today*, Lutterworth, U.K., 1949; p.92 Djiniyini Gondarra "Aboriginal Theology",*Journeying Together*, Uniting Church in Australia, 1945; p.92 and p.168 Deacon Boniface Perdjert, *Aborigines*, Catholic Commission for Justice and Peace, Australia; p.100 Mahatma Gandhi, *The Message of Christ*, publ. Bombay 1963; p.122 Herbert Jai Singh,*The Lord's Prayer*,CISRS, Bangalore, 1985; p.128 Ron O'Grady "Palm Sunday",*Ecumenical Peace Program in Asia*, Hong Kong, 1987; p.138 Miriam-Rose Ungunmerr-Baumann, *Australian Stations of the Cross*,Collins/Dove,Melbourne,1984; p.142 *Testimonies of Faith, Letters and Poems from Prison in Taiwan*, WARC, 1984 and Anne Ming *Taiwanese Voice*, British Council of Churches, 1981; p.152 Hilda Buhay,"Who is Mary?"*In God's Image*, Hong Kong, December 1989; p.154 Korean SCF, *Life in All Its Fullness*, WSCF Books No.7; p.158 Wang Weifan,*Lilies of the Field* ,tr. Janice and Philip Wickeri, FTE, Hong Kong, 1989; p.176 Edicio de la Torre,*Touching Ground, Taking Root*, SPI, Philippines, 1986.

Among the other meditations in the book are a number written specially for this publication.

Artists

Artists whose work appears in this book are listed below. The page number of their art work only is shown with information about the artist normally on the facing page. Surnames appear first. In the body of the book the traditional Chinese and Korean custom of using the surname first is preserved.

General Index

The Asian Christian Art Association

Founded in 1978 to be a forum for Christian artists in the Asian region, it has become a creative centre for professional artistic expression in the Asian churches.

The Association has conducted numerous art exhibitions at international venues and holds periodic conferences to discuss the role of Christian artists in today's Asia.

The Association's magazine, IMAGE, has been published every three months since 1978. It contains reproductions of art works and up-to-date information about art and artists in the region.

This book, "The Bible Through Asian Eyes", is the latest in a number of publications dealing with Asian Christian art. For further information on these books, or on any matter related to the work of the Association you are invited to write to:

Asian Christian Art Association
Kansai Seminar House
23 Takenouchi-cho, Ichijoji,
Sakyo-ku, Kyoto 606
JAPAN

Tel: (075) 711-2115   Fax: (075) 701-5256